Praise For Jon Haggins

"Jon Haggins is America's premier African-American travel guide. He takes readers to many places of color. In The African-American Travel Guide to Hot, Exotic & Fun-Filled Places, Haggins points out sights of particular interest in Africa, South America, the Caribbean, even Fiji. Along with insights into historic relevance, Haggins provides practical information on what to take along, necessary shots to have in advance, restaurants, hotels, etc."

—*Robert Dahlin, Publisher's Weekly*

"Up, up and away! In his one of a kind book The African American Travel Guide, travel guru Jon Haggins gives helpful tips such as how to prepare for your journey and how to have the most fun when you get there. Jon is a veteran travel host with his own television show and nationally syndicated newspaper column. He acts as the reader's personal guide through the palm dotted islands of Fiji, down the Nile pass the timeless temples, follow the rhythm of the African drum and aromas to Brazil, just to name a few of the fascinating locals offered up in his book. In addition to the vivid descriptions and witty insights those familiar with Jon's work have come to expect, there is his unique practical information and advice: What to pack: pack a bathing suit in your carry on so that you can go for a dip, in case your luggage is delayed. Also pack a four-pound box of Epsom Salt to use in your bath water. It helps to ease the pain after a long day of touring. What not to miss: Do not miss shopping in Egypt and Morocco where Jon will show you how to become an experienced haggler and get the most for your dollar. Before getting shots, applying for visas, or packing the first stitch of clothing, there is one item you must never forget to pack, "A sense of humor because it will help you get through the day." In this informative and discerning book Jon shows you how to begin your trip— and how to end it—with a smile.

—*Eric Copage, best selling author of seven books published by Hyperion and William Morrow*

"*Liberating. We wish everyone could experience the memories.*"

—*Oscar & Michelle Williams, New York City*

"**Thanks, Jon for hosting a tres magnificent Black History Month Tour to Dakar, Senegal.** *Especially the details, planning and overall sensitivity to the historical significance of our pilgrimage.*"

—*Florence James, Los Angeles, CA*

"*I truly enjoyed the Dakar experience. I've been home now for a month and rarely a day goes by when I don't think about either someone I met or some place I visited while in Senegal.* **For me, the trip was really life changing.** *I want to thank you personally for all the time and effort you put into making this trip such a success. I look forward to traveling with you again.*"

—*David Cwirka, Meriden, CT*

"**Your expertise, genuine authentic care and concern for my welfare made me feel especially comfortable in traveling as a single.** *I would recommend that other singles not postpone their travel due to the lack of a partner.*"

—*Chris Outlaw, Memphis, TN*

"*My trip to Ghana was my second with Jon within a year.* **Jon's African itineraries are well thought out and planned,** *with just the right mix for cultural and historical enlightment, photography and social interaction. I am looking forward to my next tour to Morocco with Jon.*"

—*Ron Scudder, Hackensack, NJ*

"*After waiting many years to experience Africa,* **I was amazed that it was just as I had pictured it: exotic, mysterious, warm and welcoming.** *I cannot wait to return.*"

—*Miriam Baker Wilson, New York City*

"**Jon, thank you for the opportunity to visit Senegal and Gambia;** *and thank God for life and people like my fellow voyagers.*"

—*Anita Muhammad, Chicago, IL*

"Thanks for making my trip to Senegal such an outstanding event. I will talk about it for the rest of my life. Thanks for the memory."

—Dorothy Sumpter, New York City

Five Great Reasons for Sharing **The African-American Travel Guide to Hot, Exotic and Fun-Filled Places** *by Jon Haggins*

▼ Jon paints pictures with words and allows you to come along to those many exotic destinations.

▼ Jon makes travel a colorful experience that you will never forget.

▼ Jon shares his humor and sensitivity while traveling around the world, making it an educational and fun experience while delving into many cultures.

▼ To broaden one's perspective of travel around the world.

▼ To illustrate how you can share a fun and educational experience.

The African-American Travel Guide

To Hot, Exotic, and Fun-Filled Places

By Jon Haggins

Amber Books
New York   Los Angeles
Phoenix

The African-American Travel Guide to Hot, Exotic, and Fun-Filled Places

by Jon Haggins

Published by:
Amber Books
1334 East Chandler Boulevard, Suite 5-D67
Phoenix, AZ 85048
amberbk@aol.com
www.amberbooks.com

Tony Rose, Publisher/Editorial Director   Samuel P. Peabody, Associate Publisher
Yvonne Rose, Senior Editor   The Printed Page, Interior & Cover Design

© Copyright 2002 by Jon Haggins and Amber Books
ISBN #: 0-9702224-0-8

Library of Congress Cataloging-In-Publication Data

Haggins, Jon.
    The African-American travel guide to hot, exotic, and fun-filled places / by Jon Haggins.
        p. cm.
    ISBN 0-9702224-0-8
        1. Africa--Guidebooks. 2. South America--Guidebooks. 3. Caribbean
    Area--Guidebooks. 4. Fiji--Guidebooks. African-Americans--Travel--Guidebooks. I.
    Title.

DT2.H34 2002
910'.89'96073--dc21

                                                                            2002018511

10 9 8 7 6 5 4 3 2 1
First Printing April 2002

Dedication

In Memory of my Granddad, Richard Walker, who said,

"Travel, cause travel is an education. There is a great big world out there just waiting to be devoured."

To my Mother, Willie Mae
You are the backbone of my life

About the Author

Jon Haggins is the executive director and host of GlobeTrotter with Jon Haggins™, a weekly half-hour television show. Jon is the travel and food writer for *The Amsterdam News*, *Travel & Style* magazine, and *City & Suburban Style* magazine. He has written fashion and travel articles for *Upscale* magazine and *Black Elegance* magazine. Jon is also a contributing author for Eric Copage's new book, *Soul Food* (a collection of short, inspirational stories), published by Hyperion Books.

Jon Haggins owns and operates Haggins International Tours, which offers affordable and personalized group tours to seven African countries and Brazil. Haggins International Tours editorials have appeared in *The New York Times*, *NY Newsday*, *Amsterdam News*, *The Daily News*, *The Chicago Tribune*, *Florida Today*, *The Washington Post*, *Boston Globe*, *The Bergen Record*, *The Dallas News*, *Tennessean*, *Los Angeles Times*, *Los Angeles Daily News*, *San Francisco Examiner*, *Houston Chronicle*, *Charlotte Post*, *Essence*, *Heart & Soul*, *Black Enterprise*, *and Black Elegance Magazines*, etc.

Acknowledgments

Sara Camilli, my agent and friend. I thank you for your undying
energy and making this book possible.

Tony Rose (publisher of Amber Books),
I thank you for believing and publishing this book.

Lorraine Curry, Andrea Skinner,
Carolyn & Eileen McGonigle and Mary Esta Carr,
Paulo de Santos, Victor Jones, Ted Hardin, Bob Deadmon,
Cynthia Moore, RoseAnne Forde, Chris Outlaw,
Yvonne Rose (Senior Editor, Amber Books) and
my friends who saw me through.

Ky Hackney for planting the seed.

Eric Copage & Florence DeSantis
who taught me how to write.

Contents

Introduction. African/American Travel with Style. xvii

Part 1. 1

Chapter 1. Preparations For Traveling. 3

Chapter 2. Tips For Finding Tour Operators 7

Chapter 3. Travel Insurance, Inoculations, Health and Safety Tips . 9
    What sort of insurance do you need?. 9
    If an Innoculaton is Required 10

Chapter 4. International Driver's License, Passport and
Travel Visa Information 13
    International Driver's License 13
    Passport. 13
    How to Apply for a U.S. Passport 15
    Travel Visas 18

Chapter 5. Travel Recommendations. 19

Chapter 6. How to Pack and Unpack 21
    The Key to Packing Well 22
    Unpacking Your Luggage 24
    Handy Items to Take 24
    Amortize Your Luggage 25

Chapter 7. What to Expect When You Arrive at Your Destination . 27

Chapter 8. Where to Exchange Your Money 31

Chapter 9. Bartering and Haggling in the Craft Markets 33

Chapter 10. Special Interest Tours: Suggested Ideas 37
    Church Groups 37
    Black History Month Tours 37
    Big Gals Tours 37
    Business Conferences 38
    Musical Study Groups 38
    Doctors 38
    Sports 38
    Dance 38
    Agriculture 39
    Lawyers 39
    Organizations 39
    Economic groups 39
    Sororities/Fraternities 39
    Shopping 39
    Anthropology Groupse 40

Chapter 11. Unusual Places for a Wedding/Honeymoon 41
    Suggested places for a wedding 42
    How to make your honeymoon sweet: 45
    Get help to pay for your trip: 45

Chapter 12. Most Frequently Asked Travel Questions 47

Part 2. . . . . **57**

Chapter 1. Ivory Coast: Black and Proud 59

Chapter 2. Dakar, Senegal: The Motherland. 63

Chapter 3. Roots in the Gambia—A Land Filled with History and Art. 77

Chapter 4. Accra, Ghana. 83
The Gold Coast. 83
The Slave Castles 84
Crafts and Markets 86

Chapter 5. Egypt: The Land of Pharaohs, Kings and Queens . . . 89
Spiritual Healing and Nubian Heritage in Egypt 97

Chapter 6. The Magic and Mystery of Morocco 101

Chapter 7. Adventures in South Africa 119
The Township Of Soweto 121
The Adventures of Kruger Park 122
The Rolling Hills of Umtata—Mr. Nelson Mandela's
Hometown 124
East London. 126
Cape Town—Miami's Sister City 126
Following Mandela's Footsteps to Robben's Island 128

Chapter 8. Black Heritage in Brazil. 131
Salvador 131
Bahia. 132
Rio de Janeiro 133
Salvador, Bahia Is Magical 134
Sightseeing. 137
Sampling the Local Delicacies 138
A Cultural Experience in Rio 140
Rio is more than a Beach. 142
More to See 143
Living Like the Locals 144

Chapter 9. Uruguay the Land of Dreams 147
   Small Country with a Big Heart 147
   Montevideo—Many Personalities 148
   An Estancia Adventure. 150
   Punta Del Este. 153
   Soccer by the Seaside. 154

Chapter 10. Ecuador—Cosmopolitan Cities in Ecuador 157
   An Ecological Lodge at the Basin of the Amazon 160
   Preserving the Ecological Galapagos 162

Chapter 11. The Exotic Islands of Fiji 165
   A Luxury Cruise in the Fiji Islands. 167

Chapter 12. Adventures in Puerto Rico. 171
   Discovering the Cobblestone Streets of Old San Juan. 171
   Adventures in Puerto Rico 173
   Heineken Jazz/Fest Jazz in Puerto Rico 175

Chapter 13. Turks and Caicos 179

**Chapter 14. U.S. Virgin Islands: St. John, St. Thomas,
and St. Croix** 185

Chapter 15. Jamaica—Family Run Inns 195

Chapter 16. Grenada, A Spice To Savor. 203

Appendix A. Embassies and Consulates. 207

Appendix B. Departments of Tourism 217

Appendix C. Airlines & Cruise Lines 219

Appendix D. Hotels and Resorts 221

Appendix E. Convention Centers. 223

Introduction
African/American Travel with Style

The African-American Travel Guide to Hot, Exotic and Fun-Filled Places will show you a magnificent part of the world through my eyes. You will explore the flavor of several selected countries in the magnificent worlds of Africa, Brazil and other exotic destinations while walking the lush beaches and historical paths in Gambia, Ghana, The Ivory Coast, Morocco, Senegal, Brazil, Fiji and the Caribbean. You will travel to Egypt, the land of the Pharaohs, where everything is larger than life; cruise the Nile, tour the temples; journey to the Valley of the Kings and Queens and tour the Museum of the Antiquities.

More and more people are discovering that Africa is a rich and influential world with many natural resources. With its roots in many countries, Africa has influenced the world with music, artistry and history; and contributed significantly to the fashions that we see on the streets today. African-American families of three generations who travel back and bond in Africa return to the States with a new personal center and a connection to the Motherland. Africa is a wonderful, eye opening, inspiring, exhilarating, educational, memorable and fun experience. It's food for the soul.

You will go to Brazil, which has the largest African population outside of Africa. At one time, Africans were brought to Brazil to work the cocoa plantations in Bahia. Much of their African heritage, such as religion, music, and dance has been maintained and savored. Condomble and

Umbanda (a form of Maccumba) are two religions that were brought over from Africa and are still practiced today. Carnival in Bahia and Rio de Janeiro, is a festive and colorful time of year. The Samba bands allow you to participate in the world's largest carnival. It's an experience you'll never forget. Samba is in the blood of every Brazilian.

I will take you off the beaten path to assorted and unusual places, where you'll experience intriguing excursions, such as: a midnight shopping adventure to a local factory; rappelling four-hundred feet into a cave; snorkeling in the Pacific Ocean and the Red Sea; sitting in the cockpit of a 747 plane while landing in Egypt; or riding horses on a ranch in Uruguay.

I want you to feel as if you've been to each country and mingled with the locals to learn more about their culture and traditions. I believe that travel is an educational tool that brings people together to get a better understanding of other cultures and helps people learn to accept other people for what they are. Are you ready? All packed? Well, let's go! I'll take you there…

GlobeTrotter Jon Haggins

Part 1
The Basics

Part 1
The Basics

Chapter 1
Preparations For Traveling

Don't deny yourself the trip of a lifetime. The most economical way to travel is with a group. The well-prepared traveler is a happy traveler. Put in a little extra time and thought, before you leave home and it will make the difference between a medium trip and a sensational trip.

Buying a package tour can maximize your time and money. It's the most effective means of touring a destination, especially for a first time traveler. A planned tour will allow you to do and see the maximum amount of activities in the shortest time.

It's important to start an exercise program well ahead of your planned trip. Take a yoga class, learn deep breathing. Breathing can help take away stress. Jump into your sneakers and jogging-suit and run around the block a couple times a day to get in shape. Touring is very strenuous and exhausting if you aren't in shape. If you are especially tense a Shiatsu Massage might help you relax.

Save up for your journey to a favorite destination. Try trimming something from your budget in order to raise the money for your tour—maybe eating out once a week. For instance: if a package tour cost $1,500.00, that equals $130.00 x 12 months or $33.00 per week or less than $5.00 per day. Try dropping your daily coins in a jar and by the end of the year, you will have saved enough money for a major tour. As you are doing your financial planning, remember that most tours must be paid sixty days in advance.

A package tour includes: International airfare, transfers, baggage handling, air-conditioned motorcoach, English speaking guide, deluxe hotel, tours and some meals. Your package does not include: Tips for waiters, porters, maids, drivers, guides, the cost of beverages, phone calls, laundry, valet service or souvenirs.

I spent only $200.00 of out of pocket money during a ten-day tour to Egypt, which included drinks and shopping. Everything else was included in the tour package.

Now that you're financially and physically prepared for travel, it's time to research where you're going. A good starting point for research is the library. There are many tapes, books and general information about travel destinations. Or you can surf the Internet in the comfort of your own home. Research all travel options. There are over 3,000,000 pages of destinations and interests content, offering events and listings worldwide on the Internet. Currency exchange, weather forecasts, maps, points of interest magazine, travel bargains and news updates. Cruise information and last minute deals, plus a merchandise mall.

For more information for planning your own trip, visit several sites including AOL.com, Excite.com, Yahoo.com, Netnoir.com, and travelocity.com.

Flights to Africa and other destinations are not as frequent as domestic flights. As a matter of fact, direct flights to West Africa are scheduled two or three times weekly. During the high season there are more flights scheduled. Tours to those countries are often the most reliable, economical, and safest way to travel.

▼ For information on specific countries you might wish to visit their Web page.

▼ Check the Web Sites for the official word. Many agencies of the Federal Government have pages on the Internet with information for travelers.

▼ travel.state.gov/travel_warnings.html
State Department travel warnings, announcements and information sheets for every country.

▼ travel.state.gov/passport_services.html
Information on how and where to apply for passports: includes a passport application that can be downloaded.

▼ travel.state.gov/links.html
There are links to home pages of U.S. embassies and consulates throughout the world.

▼ www.customs.ustreas.gov/travel
U.S. Custom Service regulations for returning U.S. residents.

▼ www.cdc.gov/travel/travel.html
Requirements and recommendations about vaccinations, and country-specific health information from the Centers for Disease Control and Prevention.

▼ www.bts.gov/virtually
Links from the Bureau of Transportation Statistics for home pages for airlines, airports, railways and bicycle organizations.

I will answer questions at:

      e-mail:JonHaggins@aol.com

Chapter 2
Tips For Finding Tour Operators

Research tour operators who specialize in your desired destination. Ask the Better Business Bureau for recommendations about how the operator conducts business. And how long they have been in business. The longer they have been around, the more experience they'll have.

Ask if the tour company belongs to any professional associations, such as the U.S. Tour Operators Association, ATA, National Tours Association or American Society of Travel Agents. In case of a problem, you'll have some extra clout to a complaint.

Also, ask if the tour operator accompanies the group and how often they travel to the destination. Who else has signed up for the tour? If you're single, you might not want to do a tour with couples. If you're in your 60's or 70's, a trip with 20 something's may not appeal (and vice versa)

Compare itineraries for the best value. Just because the price seems cheaper at first look, doesn't mean it is. When optional tours are added and you add it all up, it might become more expensive than an inclusive package.

What is the size of the group? Ask about the maximum (often 15-20 people in small group tours) and minimum number of participants. Some tours run with as few as six, but charge a supplement; if fewer sign up, tours may be canceled.

The only way to guarantee a roommate is to bring one. If the tour company cannot match you with a roommate, you must pay for a single-supplement.

Inquire as to what the single supplement is. Make sure you review your itinerary for what is included in the tour and check if there are any extra charges. Ask about your guide, what is his or her background? Does he speak English and several other languages? Will the guide accompany you throughout your tour? You should ask about accommodations and food. Find out specifics about provisions and the cuisine of the country you are visiting.

Look for down time or any free time on your itinerary. Some tours go at a breakneck pace. Know if you'll have time to explore on your own or just relax. You'll need to find the tour that suits your personality, interest and physical abilities.

Ask your friends about a tour operator. The best dependable recommendation comes from experience. Remember, word of mouth is the best advertising.

Chapter 3
Travel Insurance, Inoculations, Health and Safety Tips

What sort of insurance do you need?

Companies need liability insurance to protect them and you. Inquire about trip cancellation insurance, in case an emergency arises. Also, see about additional medical/emergency evacuation insurance, since most U.S. health policies won't cover you outside the country. Again, I strongly recommend full trip cancellation insurance.

When you charge your ticket on an American Express card, you are offered a $100,000.00 accident and life insurance. Global Assist® will locate an international hospital or doctor for you.

Master Card suggests you check with your bank of issuance for specific details regarding your card. They offer pre-trip information such as advisor on weather, local currency and local immunization. It's best to call your Master Card Bank to inquire about their insurance policies.

Visa Gold or Platinum Card offers $150,000.00 in life and travel accident insurance. For lost baggage they will help you find an assistant to locate your baggage. And will suggest medical locations in foreign countries. For the Classic card, there is no insurance, but they will assist with lost or stolen cards and block further usage of stolen cards. You have to pay separately for travel insurance.

You can obtain a comprehensive travel protection plan insurance from your travel agent. Your travel insurance covers: trip cancellation/interruption protection, emergency medical, dental coverage, emergency medical transportation, baggage coverage, baggage delay, vacation delay, travel accident, trip inconvenience, collision/loss damage benefit (optional) and 24-hour hotline assistance. However the maximum amount of trip cancellation/interruption coverage is $20,000.00.

Blue Cross-Blue Shield now applies overseas

The Blue Cross and Blue Shield plans have begun a program to enable many holders of their medical insurance to use selected hospitals in Europe, Japan, Israel, Mexico and a total of forty countries around the world. The Blue Cardholder would be treated as if they were going to a hospital at home. Instead of the patient's paying the whole cost on departure and filing for reimbursement, the foreign hospital will bill the Blue Cross-Blue Shield plan directly and the patients will be responsible only for the extra charges they would pay at home: co-payments, non-covered services and deductibles.

Eligible holders have cards with identification numbers preceded by a letter or letters. They may hold the insurance through a plan at work or many people purchase it independently. Blue Cross-Blue Shield said that at least 85 percent of their 74 million policyholders have access to the overseas benefit.

There are one hundred-forty hospitals in 40 countries around the world that accept your Blue Card (Blue Cross/Blue Shield)

For more information: 1-800-810-BLUE or www.bluecares.com

If An Innoculaton Is Required

A Yellow fever vaccination certificate is required for all travelers over one year of age to a number of African countries. The Yellow fever inoculation lasts for ten years. We also strongly recommend you ask your doctor for a prescription for Malarial suppressants (Lariam) to prevent Malaria fever from a possible mosquito bite. The Malarial suppressant is taken orally once a week, starting one week before departure and continue for five consecutive weeks on the same day.

Yellow Fever vaccination, immunizations and Malaria Pills may be obtain from your family doctor, the U.S. Department of Health or:

Executive Health Group
10 Rockefeller Plaza
New York City 10020
212-486-8900

International Health Care Service
440 E. 69th Street
New York City 10021
212-746-1601
212-746-8978-fax

Traveler's Medical
2141 K Street NW, Suite 408
Washington, DC
202-466-8109

Chapter 4
International Driver's License, Passport and Travel Visa Information

International Driver's License

AAA members can obtain an international driver's license at your local AAA office. You must present your current license accompanied by two 2 x 2 photos. AAA plus members will receive a free international driver's license, the basic member, must pay $6.00 and a non-member $10.00.

Passport

Your country as a form of identification issues a Passport. A passport is your proof of citizenship of the country you claim. And it allows you permission to exit and enter your country. The turn around time for a new or renewed passport is approximately three weeks from the day you apply.

You can request a faster service for receiving your Passport, Visa or International Driver's License within a week, 48 hours, next day or same day, through Passport Plus, Inc at 20 East 49th St (3rd floor) New York City 10017...212-759-5540 or 1-800-367-1818-voice or fax 212-759-5805. They provide service for all the States.

While traveling, it's handy to wear a waist pouch under your clothing so that it doesn't flash tourist. A waist pouch can be purchased at most novelty or luggage stores. They are made in canvas cloth or leather, price from $10.00 and up. It comes in a standard size to accommodate your passport, immunization papers, boarding pass, airline ticket, credit cards, money, and traveler's checks. Copy the first page of your passport for identification and carry it in a different place other than your pouch. It's also a good idea to leave a copy with a friend at home so it can be faxed if necessary. It saves a lot of time and trouble if your passport is lost.

Your passport is the most valuable document you own when you are visiting another country. The purpose of the passport is to allow you entry and exit to and from the United States. The passport is not the easiest document to replace when you're away from home. If you should happen to misplace your passport, go immediately to the American Embassy. Remember the pace of other countries is sometimes a bit slower than in the States.

You may obtain a passport from your local post office, passport agency or Passport Plus. You can also download a passport form from the Internet at http://www.travel.state.gov.

You can also order your passport by mail, but only if you already have one that was issued within the past 12 years and you are over 18. Obtain form DSP-82 (passport by mail) and send it to:

> National Passport Center
> PO Box 371971
> Pittsburgh, PA 15250-7971

Or visit by appointment only:

> Passport Office
> 376 Hudson St.
> New York City, NY 10013

For overnight delivery, send your package to:

> Mellon Bank
> Attn: Passport Supervisor 371971
> 3 Mellon Bank Center, RM 153-2723
> Pittsburgh, PA 15259-0001

Remember to include the appropriate fee for overnight return of your passport. In other words, if you're using FedEx, DHL, Next Day or Two-Day Mail at the Post Office or UPS. Make sure you include an extra Airbill in the envelope along with a form of payment. If you travel frequently, you can request a forty-eight-page passport at the time of application. An adult passport is good for ten years, therefore you have to decide how much international travel you will be doing that will warrant a regular or 48 page passport.

Check with the embassy or consulate of the countries that you plan to visit for entry requirements. Some countries require that your passport be valid at least 6 months beyond the dates of your trip. You don't want it to expire while you're there.

How to Apply for a U.S. Passport

U.S. passports are issued only to U.S. Citizens or Nationals (person born abroad, but has obtained U.S. Citizenship). Each person must obtain his or her own passport.

If you're a first time applicant, you must complete and submit an application in person. (Applicants under 13 years of age usually need not appear in person unless requested. A parent or guardian may execute the application on the child's behalf.) Each application must be accompanied by:

(1) Proof of U.S. Citizenship,

(2) Proof of Identity,

(3) Two photographs, photos can be obtained from a local photo shop for approximately $10.00 to $12.00.

4) Fees (as explained below) to one of the following acceptance agents: a clerk of any Federal or State court accepting applications; a designated postal employee at a selected post office; or an agent at a Passport Agency in Boston, Chicago, Honolulu, Houston, Los Angeles, Miami, New Orleans, New York, Philadelphia, San Francisco, Seattle, Stamford, or Washington, DC; or a U.S. consular official.

If you have had a previous passport, inquire about eligibility to use Form DSP-82 (mail-in application). Address requests for passport amendment, extension of validity, or additional visa pages to a Passport Agency or a U.S. Consulate or Embassy abroad. Check visa requirements with consular officials of countries to be visited well in advance of your departure.

(1) Proof of U.S. Citizenship:

(a) Applicants born in the United States. Submit previous U.S. Passport or certified birth certificate. A birth certificate must include your given name and surname, date and place of birth, date the birth record was filed, and seal or other certification of the official custodian of such records. A record filed more than one year after the birth is acceptable if it is supported byevidence described in the next paragraph.

If no birth record exists, submit the Registrar's notice to that effect. Also submit an early baptismal or circumcision certificate, hospital birth record, early census, school or family Bible records, newspaper article on your birth (preferably with at least one record listed above). Evidence should include your given name and surname, date and place of birth, and seal or other certification of office (if customary) and signature of issuing official.

(b) Applicants born outside the United States. Submit previous U.S. Passport or Certificate of Naturalization, or Certificate of Citizenship, or a Report of Birth Abroad, or evidence described below.

If you claim citizenship through naturalization of parent(s), submit a Consular Report of Birth (Form FS-240) or certification of Birth (Form DS-1350 or FS-545), or your foreign birth certificate, parents' marriage certificate, proof of citizenship of your parents(s), and affidavit of U.S. citizen parent(s) showing all periods and places of residence/physical presence in the United States and abroad before your birth.

(2) Proof of Identity.

If you are not personally known to the acceptance agent, you must establish your identity to the agent's satisfaction. You may submit items such as the following containing your signature and physical description or photograph that is a good likeness of you: previous U.S. passport: Certificate of Naturalization or of Citizenship: drivers license (not temporary or learner's license): or government (Federal, State, municipal) identification card or pass. Temporary or altered documents are not acceptable.

If you cannot prove your identity as stated above, you must appear with an identifying witness who is a U.S. citizen or permanent resident alien who has known you for at least two years. Your witness must prove his or her identity and complete and sign an Affidavit of Identifying Witness (Form DSP-71) before the acceptance agent. You must also submit some identification of your own.

(3) Two photographs.

Submit two identical photographs of you alone, sufficiently recent to be a good likeness (normally taken within the last 6 months), 2 x 2 inches in size, with an image size from bottom of chin to top of head (including hair) of between 1 and 13/8 inches.

Photographs must be clear, front view, full face, taken in normal street attire without a hat or dark glasses, and printed on thin paper with a plain light(white or off-white) background.

They may be black and white or color. They must be capable of withstanding a mounting temperature of 225 degrees Fahrenheit (107degrees Celsius). Photographs retouched so that your appearance is changed are unacceptable. Snapshots, most vending machine prints, and magazine or full-length photographs are unacceptable.

(4) Fees:

Submit $65.00 if you are 18 years of age or older. The passport fee is $55.00. In addition, a fee of $10.00 is charged for the execution of the application. Your passport will be valid for ten years from the date of issue. Submit $40.00 if you are under 18 years of age. The passport fee is $30.00 and the execution fee is $10.00.Your passport will be valid for five years from the date of issue, except where limited as above.

Pay the passport and execution fees in one of the following forms: checks —personal, certified, or traveler's; bank draft or cashier's check; money order, U.S. Postal, international, currency exchange; or if abroad, the foreign currency equivalent, or a check drawn on a U.S. bank.

Make passport and execution fees payable to: Passport Services (except if applying at a State court, pay execution fee as the State court requires) or the appropriate Embassy or Consulate, if abroad. No fee is charged to applicants with U.S. Government or military authorization for no-fee passports (except State courts may collect the execution fee). Pay special postage if applicable.

Travel Visas

The country you are visiting issues a Visa. The Visa allows you permission to enter and exit their country. There is a nominal cost for a Visa that is paid to the consulate of the country you desire to visit. Check with your travel agent or local consulate of your desired destination. You can also explore the Internet for more information regarding Visas.

The cost of a visitor's Visa is subject to change, so it's best that you check with the tourist board or consulate of the country you plan to visit. When you're in another country, and decide after you're there, to take a side trip to another country that requires a Visa. You should contact the Consulate of your desired destination. See Embassies and Consulates on page 207.

Chapter 5
Travel Recommendations

You should be concerned about different bacteria in the country (or countries) you plan to visit. Therefore, I suggest you take a laxative to flush your system two days before you depart in order to reduce the conflict of bacteria. Or you will spend lots of time in the bathroom, paying the price. I feel naked if I don't carry a bottle of Citrus Magnesia, Pepto-Bismol, Mylanta or other stomach aids, just in case something goes wrong. After all, there are no local drug stores next to your hotel. Besides, you don't want to spend your precious time stumbling around looking for a drug store. Also take a box of band aids and cotton balls, alcohol, peroxide, condoms (if you're single), a box of raisons or a snicker to give you a burst of energy in the middle of touring. Pack a travel clock to assure you prompt wakeup to start your day. Shoe polish to keep your shoes shined to make the right impression. Remember a happy traveler is the best traveler. Preparing yourself with these items will ensure that you will enjoy your trip.

Another suggestion: eat a container of yogurt each day before traveling in order to build up bacteria in your stomach. Yogurt, will line your stomach with cultures to fight off foreign bacteria, which may cause an upset stomach. If you should have a case of diarrhea while traveling, take a laxative in the early evening to avoid a disruption of your daily schedule or several shots of Grand Marnier, or Black Berry Brandy—my favorite. The liquor will kill anything that steps in its way. Drinking any of the above will release whatever is upsetting your stomach. Each morning, take a swig of

Pepto-Bismol, just to play it safe. Remember, when you return home, take another laxative to flush your system again.

Avoid tap water, ice, ice cream, yogurt and any dairy products when you travel. Also, don't eat salads and fruit that are not peeled. Eat only cooked vegetables and drink bottled water that you purchase in the hotel or at a local store.

Don't wear cologne or perfume (it attracts mosquitoes).

Your tour is what you make it. Relax and get into the mode of the people of the land. Don't be uptight and expect everything to be the same as at home. Fuhgetaboutit...you're not at home. Share a cup of hibiscus tea and play dominos with the locals. Talk with them; it will give you a better understanding of their culture.

Don't be afraid to travel as a single. Tour participants come from all around the country. All have a common bond to travel to the Motherland and learn about their heritage. Touring with a group is a great way to meet a life long friend. Just like in "The Love Boat," people have even fallen in love on tours and ultimately have married.

In many West African countries it is not polite to shake with your left hand, because the left hand is used for sanitary purposes and it is only rinsed. Generally, the local toilets don't supply toilet paper. Their custom is that they only rinse their hands after cleaning themselves. A roll of toilet paper and a bar of soap are very handy to take with you. It is definitely a "no, no" to eat with your left hand. At the dinner table a pitcher of water and a sprinkle of soap is passed around, in order to wash hands before eating. Everyone gathers around a table and eats from one plate. The food is served on one platter and everyone picks a portion with his or her hands. A left-handed person is given a fork or spoon.

Chapter 6
How to Pack and Unpack

Pack a good sense of humor and lots of patience. You should be able to laugh at yourself; the world is not going to end tomorrow. Remember you're not at home. You will be meeting people from a different culture. The pace may be a bit slower, so just chill.

The electric current in Africa and Brazil is 220 direct. You may consider buying an adapter (it converts the electric current from 220 to 110 volts). An electric adapter can be purchased at most electrical supply outlets or at a dime store. An adapter is used to re-charge your batteries or plug in your iron. You may also ask your hotel for an electrical adapter. Some hotels may make them available to you. Every four or five star hotel has a valet service, but it's very expensive. You may ask the housekeeping service for an iron, but who wants to spend their holiday pressing wrinkles?

Check the Weather Reports

Check the weather reports in newspapers, on TV or on the Internet. Generally, Africa and Brazil have tropical weather. Dress casually; pack lots of 100% cotton T-shirts and jeans (you can wear jeans again and again and the dirt won't show); sneakers and good walking shoes, because you're gonna walk your little tootsies off.

Baggage Allowance

▼ **Check bags for Coach, Business and First Class:**
2 suitcases with 62 inches each (height + depth + length). Each suitcase should be no more than 70 lbs., with a total of no more than 140 lbs.

▼ **Carry-on bags:**
Each passenger should carry one carry-on bag, which should be accommodated underneath the seat or in the compartment above the seat.

The Key to Packing Well

Make a list and try to minimize your packing. You should coordinate colors, eliminate unnecessary clothing and accessories. Somehow clothes seem to magically multiply when its time to re-pack. Never fill your luggage to the maximum. Visualize each day and what you really think you will need. You'll be less harried if you're not worrying about how to fit everything into your luggage at each stop on the tour.

Lay your clothing on your bed before packing. If you've failed to limit your choices, the sight of giant piles of sweaters, skirts, shorts, shirts and slacks should bring you to your senses. Weed out whatever is unnecessary. EDIT, EDIT, EDIT. After all, you are not modeling in a fashion show. The key to packing well, is planning ahead.

Pack clothing from heaviest to the lightest. Start at the bottom of your bag, and work your way up. If you have wrinkle-prone garments, place them on top. For a long trip, pack according to itinerary: clothing for the first stop on top and the last stop on the bottom.

To aid selection, divide your list into categories, such as pants, dresses (or slacks), jackets, sweaters, shirts (T-shirts), intimate apparel (including socks and stockings), shoes, accessories (jewelry, belts and scarves) and disposable shavers, curling and travel iron). A list is useful and can be handy if your luggage is lost and you must identify contents.

Prepare your clothing at least a week before departure. Be sure your garments are laundered or dry-cleaned. Sew buttons on, hem dresses and resole your shoes-before you depart. Stuff socks and stockings into your shoes. You'll economize on space and have instant built in shoetrees. On your way home, stuff sneakers and good walking shoes with rolled items of laundry. Shoes and socks can also cushion small items, such as costume jewelry. Don't flash gold jewelry or diamonds. Wear only faux jewelry. Wear your heaviest shoes on the plane to avoid the extra weight. Lighter shoes are easier to carry.

Take a roll of bubble wrap to protect your gifts from breakage, cord or string to tie your packages and of course, bring along tape to close packages. Pack an extra collapsible canvas bag to bring home souvenirs.

Pack Clothes on Hangers

To economize on space, place several articles on each hanger. Also consider the hangers. Use plastic-bag ties to secure hangers and prevent garments from being tossed around. Remember, if your suitcase has inner ties, place tissue paper underneath them before tying them to avoid wrinkles. Also, don't close luggage until the last minute before departing in-order to avoid wrinkles.

How Long at Each Destination

Take stock of the length of time you'll spend at each destination. How many business and pleasure encounters do you plan to have, whether formal, informal, daytime or evening? How many changes of clothing do you require per day? Are you a one T-shirt per day person or do you require more frequent changes?

Banishing Wrinkles

Even the best packer has to contend with wrinkled clothing on occasion. To banish creases, or contend with them, here are a few tips:

Place plastic dry cleaner's bags between garments. This is as good a technique for preventing wrinkles, as using sheets of tissue paper. Rolling is a great space saver for conventional suitcases, too. Roll pants from the hem to waist in-order to avoid wrinkles; do the same for T-shirts. This works especially well in duffel bags, where the most crushable pieces should be on the inside. Use airline slippers, regular plastic bags or conventional shoe bags for shoes. Aside from keeping your shoe polish from soiling clothing, this helps keep stuffed items from falling out.

Unpacking Your Luggage

When you arrive at your hotel or destination, unpack as quickly as possible to avoid any unnecessary wrinkles. Be sure to hang your crushables. Place a wet towel over a hanger and hang it in the closet with your clothes. This technique should help the wrinkles fall out. You can also stretch your garments out over the bed and use your hands to ease the wrinkles out. Whenever I have unnecessary wrinkles, I simply spread the item on the bed and lay on it for a minute or two. That way, I accomplish two missions: I get a cat-nap and relax the wrinkles.

If nothing else works, I try the old hot shower routine—turning on the hot water and giving the clothing a blast of steam, then letting it hang for a short while. From experience, I don't recommend that you try this on silk fabrics. Silk tends to shrink with steam. I had an instance in Brazil where I put a silk shirt, size 15 ½" neck and 35" sleeve in the steam. When I returned, the shirt had become about four sizes smaller.

Handy Items to Take

Take your personal medications, Kaeopectate, Pepto-Bismol, Antacid tablets, Cortizone 100 creme, Band Aids, Aspirins, shoe polish, insect repellent, Suntan lotion, makeup, bathing suit, robe, sandals for the beach or pool, Epsom Salts (for bathing after a hectic day of touring), laxative, handy wipes, toothbrush and paste, dental floss, Visine, mouthwash, tissues, bar of soap, and a roll of toilet paper (for when you're out touring). One hundred single dollar bills for tips. Include a box of raisins, M&M's, Chocolate bar and hard candy or peanuts for an instant energy snack. With your camera bring lots of film, because it is very expensive in other countries, and don't forget to bring extra batteries for the camera. The usual measure is one roll per day. However, if you're a real film buff, you might require three rolls per day.

In my carry on bag, I always pack an extra pair of prescription glasses, travel clock, batteries, amenities and other breakables. I label my luggage with my name, address, phone and e-mail number. I also suggest not buying black baggage, because it's not distinguishable. And someone may walk off with it by mistake. But, if you already own black luggage, use a bright red ribbon or red tape for easy identification. Invest in a lock for each piece of luggage. Two smaller suitcases are usually easier to manage than one large one. And wheels on luggage make traveling much more enjoyable.

Gifts and Trading

Save a corner of your suitcase for baseball caps, T-shirts, jeans, sunglasses, watches, CD players, sneakers, cosmetics, inexpensive Walkman, designer perfumes and colognes, lipsticks, calculators and watches for trading in the craft markets in West Africa. This could include clothing in your closet that you haven't worn in the past two years.

Pack Sample Size Toiletries

You'll often find your favorite cologne, soap, toothpaste and cosmetics in small sizes, at a low cost, or as giveaways—perfect for traveling. The classic alternative is to fill small plastic bottles, but not to the top. If you use plastic bottles, squeeze the sides of the containers before sealing to help avoid spillage. Keep your toilet kit, packed at all times. Replenish your supply of toiletries after each trip.

Toiletries can be bought in foreign lands, but they are expensive and drug stores are not as convenient as in the States. Many deluxe hotels provide amenities such as soap, body lotion, shower caps, shampoo and sewing kits. But if you prefer a specific brand, bring it.

Amortize Your Luggage

When you travel with a group, you can consolidate the baggage weight, especially when you return with too many gifts, so you won't have to pay for over-weight. Not everyone in your group will be shopaholics. The group is checked in at the same time and the total weight of the group allows you to return home with extra baggage. Otherwise you would have to pay for extra baggage weight. Remember, when you're buying souvenirs, wood carvings bear a lot of weight. Think sparingly. U.S. Customs allows you $450.00 per person in purchases before a tax is imposed.

Chapter 7
What to Expect When You Arrive at Your Destination

If you're traveling on a tour, your English speaking guide and assistants will greet your group at the destination airport. They will assist you through customs and collect your luggage, then escort you by air-conditioned transfer bus to your deluxe hotel. At the hotel, you will receive a welcome drink and an orientation. During the orientation, you can ask any questions to assist with learning the lay of the land.

When you first arrive, the guide will collect your airline ticket to reconfirm your return flight reservation. He will hold them until your departure. It is also common for a hotel to request to hold your passport until your departure.

If you're traveling to a country that speaks another language, go to your local bookstore or library before leaving to get a book that will give the basic words, phrases and pronunciations. There are many audio tapes on every language. Learn two useful expressions each day, one in the morning and one in the afternoon.

Helpful phrases would include how to ask for:

▼ The name of your guide(s)

▼ Your room number and for a key

▼ A safe deposit box to store your valuables. (When you get your safe deposit box, remember the number of the box. Tuck the safe key in a secret place; the cost of a lost key is $100.00 to $500.00)

▼ Practice ordering food in the restaurants. Learn the words for breakfast, lunch, and dinner and of course, drinks. It's vitally important to be able to order a bottle of water.

Other helpful phrases:

▼ How much does it cost?

▼ The name of your hotel

▼ How to ask for the bill.

▼ The bill is not correct

▼ How to order a taxi and give the driver an address

▼ How do you use the telephone?

▼ Asking for locations you want to visit

▼   A simple greeting, such as "hello" and "how are you?"

▼ Asking for the location of the swimming pool

▼ Ask about shopping in the boutiques, discos, and night clubs

▼ Asking for towels for your room.

▼ Learn how to count your money in French

If traveling with a group or on your own, have the ground operator re-confirm your return plane reservations immediately upon your arrival at your destination. Flights are often far apart and you don't want to be stranded without a reservation.

Lock valuables in hotel safe immediately. Only carry what you think you'll spend for the day. Remember, your hotel is only a taxi ride away. Dress down and don't flash expensive gold or diamond jewelry. You can't be too cautious when traveling to another country.

Americans are recognized as tourists in every market and will be approached by merchants to purchase souvenirs. The merchants know that Americans are big shoppers.

A useful Wolof expression I used in Senegal was "Byemma," which means, "Leave me alone."

You don't want to feel trapped when traveling with a group. The more adventurous traveler might want to break away from the planned meals and tours to personalize his or her tour. Go off the beaten path for a personal adventure.

Always talk with the bartenders and the piano players at your hotel. They can advise you of all the special and inexpensive spots in town. They know the lay of the land and can be very instrumental in making your holiday more eventful, exciting, educational and memorable. It's a short cut to learning about their culture.

Treat people with kindness and respect and you'll get a lot in return. The locals have introduced me to a world of fabulous places that I could never have known without them and other tourists only dream about. I was introduced to restaurants, nightclubs, museums and special shopping spots. Often they accompany me and haggle for the best price for me at the markets.

Often tourists will stick together, traveling in packs and only conversing amongst themselves. Not a good idea. Spread your wings; talk with the locals, and find out how they feel, what they think. What is the point of traveling if you don't open your mouth, mind and eyes? Traveling opens a whole New World of knowledge and experience. Travel also exposes everyone to other cultures and customs.

Chapter 8
Where to Exchange Your Money

You can exchange money at Thomas Cook (Thomas Cook is a currency exchange store) or at your local bank in the States, but that's a waste of time and you won't get a good rate of exchange. Why not exchange your money at the airport, hotel or a bank when you arrive at your destination.

If you are carrying cash, please take dollar bills in small denominations from $5.00 to $20.00 to insure an easy exchange. Also carry fifty one dollar bills for tipping. Tipping in U.S. currency makes it easier for you to comprehend the value.

I always exchange money at my hotel to save time. The hotel gives a shorter rate, but it's just a difference of a few pennies. Sometimes, I ask the guide to have money exchanged in the 'White Market,' where I received a higher rate. Another location to exchange money is at a local bank, where I had to fill out papers, show my passport, chew several sticks of gum and waste a lot of valuable time standing in a long, long line. I was on a limited time frame and time is very valuable. The exchange rate in the bank may be ten cents more.

Do not exchange money with someone you don't know, because it could be counterfeit. Foreign currency is different in color and size. When you arrive at your destination, spend a little time getting familiar with it. I always have to look twice at each denomination before giving or receiving an exchange. Basically people are honest, but you just want to check yourself. A 10,000 CFA note in Senegal could be easily mistaken for a 1,000 CFA note. CFA (Financial African Community) represents the currency of Senegal and Ivory Coast.

When I arrive at my destination, I always exchange $100.00 at the hotel. Remember you'll only need mad money for shopping and a few meals. The worst scenario is to end up with local currency at the end of your tour. To exchange local currency into American dollars, you lose again. If you plan on returning anytime soon, you may just want to hold on to your money. But the currency rate fluctuates daily and you never know what the rate will be, so it's usually best to get rid of what you don't need.

You can purchase travelers' checks before your departure. Credit cards and traveler checks are widely accepted in hotels and at many upscale businesses. You can use your credit card to settle up any incidental purchases at the hotel. In order to cash a traveler's check outside of your hotel, you must carry your passport for identification. Again, take special care of your money, valuables and papers.

Chapter 9
Bartering and Haggling in the Craft Markets

The Soumbedioune Market in Dakar, Senegal is located along the cornice lining the Atlantic Ocean. It's comprised of a cluster of vendors in an open-air market. It's a popular place for tourists. Here, I purchased leather bags, wallets, belts, woodcarvings and several masks to display on my walls when I returned home. I also bought batiks of various sizes to frame and hang. Batiks document different stories of the daily life in a village and its harvest. Across the street from the Soumbedioune Market is a collection of shops with antique carvings of statues of various sizes. I couldn't resist buying a large wooden statue that is perfect for my entrance hallway. Also, along the Atlantic coastline, men are busy carving furniture on the street.

First, ask "How much for the item?" Then do the old flinch game. Think long and hard about it. Generally the vendors ask what you want to pay. Make a slow offer of one-third or half the asking price and stick to it. The vendor will say, "That was my first price; give me your best price." That calls for some serious negotiating. If the vendor doesn't agree, then walk away. Walk away several times, until he's convinced that you don't want the item. That's when acting comes into play. You must be convincing. You pay only what you want or…fuhgetaboutit.

Bartering and haggling in the markets is a cultural thing in many countries. I even haggled in a shop at the airport in Ecuador. It's my favorite thing to do; it's an obsession.

Most Americans feel threatened or intimidated by haggling over a price. Bartering is a way of life, and it helps to understand the nuances of the culture. It's another way of building a kinship. It takes time to understand the process of bartering; it can be fun, but exhausting until you get the knack.

There are three sure steps to clinching a deal:

1. Shop alone, far away from the distraction of other tourists

2. Never pay the asking price. Generally speaking, you can bargain for one third. It can take up to an hour to negotiate for one item. After negotiating, I always throw in a little gift of a T-shirt, cologne, etc. It's my way of giving back.

3. Walk away if the seller isn't willing to entertain your offer. The old walk away trick distinguishes you from the inexperienced barterer. Remember, you don't need any of these wonderful, beautiful, irresistible items…but you want them.

Vendors will call you back to negotiate because they want to sell. I always take my tradeables in a canvas bag, because canvas won't weight me down. I never show everything at once. I tease them with one item at a time. They always ask, "Do you have something to trade?" Then point to their eye, following to your bag. "Can I see what you've got?" Remember, when you give a little with a smile, you get a lot.

A sign of an inexperienced shopper in Africa is one who doesn't understand the process of bargaining. Ask the vendor for his price, knowing you can reduce it by one third. Remember, give a little and everyone is happy.

If you're not happy with the deal, retrieve your tradeables and walk away. Then again if the merchandise is irresistible, "a must have," I suggest "Let's remain friends; I'll just pay cash money for these items." That always makes the vendor very happy—to see cold cash.

There was a collection of beautiful woven baskets just outside of my hotel. The seller wanted $65.00, and then asked what my best price was.

"$15.00" was my response. "No, that's too small," he answered. "What is your best, best price?" "$14.00," I answered. No it's too, too small. The vendor finally agreed to $15.00 under the conditions that I not tell the other tourist, who had just paid $25.00 for a smaller basket. The moment I entered the bus, I shouted, "I paid $15.00 for my basket."

After paying admission to the IFAN museum, a tourist and I only had U.S. dollars left. At the close of our personalized tour, the tourist suggested we return to the hotel to get more CFA. "No way," I stated. "Let's just go to the Soumbedioune Market and I'm sure someone will exchange our dollars for the taxi fare." I left her in the cab as ransom for the driver. I was right. A vendor friend in the market was delighted to help. The same vendor assisted in the purchase of an antique mask from another vendor, who quoted $150.00. "I don't have that kind of money," I responded. "What is your best price?" she asks, "$20.00 if she lends me the $20.00." I won the bid and landed the deal for $23.00, then was treated to a coke. Building a good relationship with people all around the world is a valuable asset.

Throughout Africa, haggling is the way of life in the craft markets and souks (a large collection of markets that sell everything from house ware to clothing).

Chapter 10
Special Interest Tours:
Suggested Ideas

Church Groups

A Church group can share an exhilarating experience of having their minister give a sermon in a Church on Goree Island, Senegal, West Africa. I anticipate your minister making references to your maiden passage to the Motherland and all its history. After the sermon, a lecture in the Slave House on the Slave Trade Route, and then a visit the Museum of History. Perhaps visit a Mosque and please don't forget Pink Lake. The lake really is pink because chemicals on the bottom reflect the light and turns the water pink).

Black History Month Tours

To learn about the African culture and the history of the Slave Trade and dress in an African Boubou (caftan) at the farewell dinner.

Big Gals Tours

Cruises are a wonderful way to relax and share a good time with your friends. When you cruise, you only pack once. Cruise lines offer lots of amenities and it's all-inclusive.

Business class seats are larger and more comfortable for you during your flight. You want to arrive as rested as possible. Dakar is on the Atlantic Ocean and fresh seafood is a part of their staple diet and helps trim the waistline. Eating healthy and exercising is the routine of the day. One hour of exercise class and several laps in the pool or simple water aerobics. (Can't forget the cultural tours for more exercise). Touring is strenuous and exhausting. Put on your sneakers and jogging pants and run along the panoramic cornice to shape up.

Business Conferences

Combines government, business, media etc. Its a full eight days of conferences and culture to get people together from Fortune 500 companies from across the United States and Africa. Meet once a year to exchange ideas and discuss how to join forces and help make business better and more fruitful for everyone.

Musical Study Groups

Bring Jazz and the Blues to Africa. Musical groups join forces to learn more about the drum and other African and Brazilian instruments. Musical study groups from colleges can learn the intricate rhythms of Africa and Brazil. After all, Brazil is a direct derivative of Africa and the beat and sound remain strong.

Doctors

Learn more about natural herbs or alternative medicine. Witness a ceremony with an herbal doctor or Voodoo Man. Learn how to incorporate modern medicine with natural herbal cures of roots, plants and trees and the natural remedies they process. Visit a local hospital to exchange medical ideas with doctors and nurses.

Sports

Participate in a soccer show off, a wrestling or swim match.

Dance

African dance companies can integrate with African/American dance companies to exchange their dance techniques and skills. Learn the essence of each movement. Have a dance competition.

Agriculture

American Agricultural groups joining forces to plant trees for prosperity. African/Americans can learn how to plant food and rotate crops. Gain knowledge regarding different kinds of foods and plants and irrigation systems.

Lawyers

Arrange to meet with other people of the judicial system. Learn the workings of each country and compare policy. Lend advice to help strengthen the bond between Africans and African/Americans.

Organizations

Organizations who want to join together to make a difference. Perhaps get corporate sponsorship for African/American students to visit or share an exchange program. They can run a clothing drive to bring new and used clothing to the villages, or bring their knowledge and skills of mass production to teach the Africans how to mass-produce their products.

Economic groups

Bankers and economists meet with comparable groups to learn more about the economic value and workings of each country. They can share knowledge of how to start an investment club. Meet with delegates and ministers from each country.

Sororities/Fraternities

Club groups interested in establishing a relationship with African countries. They might raise funds to build a community and exchange student program or help strengthen the African resources. The sororities/fraternities will appoint members of its organization to meet with their affiliates.

Shopping

Shop 'til you drop in the many craft and fabric markets. Shop for unbelievable printed cottons, leather goods, baskets and wood carvings. Visit various factories; observe teenagers making embroideries on fashionable African Boubou.

Stroll along the boulevard to soak up the fashions. Purchase an African Boubou from a local shop for approximately $35.00 or have it custom made for $65.00. There are unbelievable printed fabrics just waiting to belong to you.

Anthropology Groups

Visit Egypt for a mind blowing historical tour accompanied by a local Egyptologist. A group can explore the many temples and tombs with the Egyptologist. And visit the Valley of the Kings and Queens.

Chapter 11
Unusual Places for a Wedding/Honeymoon

Africa, is five times the size of the United States and has fifty-three countries and at least that many locations for your spectacular wedding. Come celebrate your wedding/honeymoon in Africa. Thinking about an unusual wedding location? Well, we've got several locations for your choosing. A Nubian wedding celebration while cruising the Nile River in Egypt or a wedding in a church on Goree Island in Senegal. Your wedding will be an everlasting memory and a sensational celebration for your family, lover and friends. Remember, a wedding is a very special occasion for you and that very exceptional person in your life. It's your wedding day and you want to get the most out of the occasion. You want the memories to last a lifetime. After all this is not something you plan to do again (soon).

Take advantage of a once in a lifetime experience and share your wedding day in Africa or any of the exotic destinations included in this book. Each country has its own culture and tradition and I'm sure you will want to incorporate some of their customs in your affair. A usual wedding celebration, will be an event that will last forever in your memories.

A tour company can plan a wedding package that includes:
- ▼ Airfare
- ▼ Transfers
- ▼ Baggage handling
- ▼ Air-conditioned motorcoach
- ▼ Deluxe hotel
- ▼ English speaking guides
- ▼ Meals and tours as specified on your itinerary.
- ▼ You can request flowers, cake and a minister. Special requests need to be arranged far in advance.

Suggested places for a wedding

Senegal

Goree Island wedding in a church, then a lecture on the Slave trade and a visit to the Historical Museum. Polish off the day with a reception in a restaurant overlooking the sea.

> Take your bridal party on a four-wheel drive on the most extraordinary palm shaded, white sand beach with pure aqua and turquoise blue waters and great white swells. If you feel really tropical, perhaps you might consider a wedding at the 300 foot pool at the Savanna Hotel in Dakar (a five star hotel) where tall palm trees stand erect while the African sun beams though the leaves.

The Lagune II Restaurant is the most extraordinary sight in all Dakar. The restaurant is built on an extended pier overlooking Goree Island.

At the re-naming and farewell dinner, you'll dress in your African Boubous, re-new your vows or share your wedding ceremony with your fellow travelers. It's a deep-rooted celebration of your acceptance of your new African name. At the occasion, there is entertainment with dancers and African talking drums. Plus a Marabout (High Priest, spiritual leader) will give you an African name and confirm it with a document.

Gambia

A wedding at the Atlantic Beach Hotel, directly on the beach overlooking the Banjul River. Visit the markets, museum and Mamma Tie-Dye. Mamma Tie-Dye is a factory that produces beautiful tie-dye cloth and batiks.

Ghana

Visit the city of Accra, Kumasi (home of the Ashanti Kingdom). Imagine a wedding in the Elmina Slave Castle in the Central Region and have your reception on the beach at the Coconut Grove Hotel.

Morocco

A wedding in the Maumounia Hotel is an extraordinary experience. You will be in the lap of luxury in a five-star hotel where Kings, Queens and movie stars have slept. Visit the Imperial Cities and Agadir to relax on the honey colored beach sand.

Egypt

The land of the Pharaohs, Kings and Queens. Have a Nubian wedding, while cruising up the Nile. Visit the Temples, Pyramids, Sakkara, Memphis, and Museum of Antiquities.

Appropriate private rooms are available for your occasion. This is a very elegant and special setting.

A wedding at the Old Cataract Hotel in Aswan at the foot of the Nile is extraordinary. The hotel represents Old World charm and elegance.

Just a few stone steps down from the hotel is a collection of feluccas that you can rent and peacefully sail the Nile. Don't forget to stop and have hibiscus tea and play dominos with the locals.

For a very special mammoth size wedding, take an extended cruise down the Nile and Lake Nazar in Abul Simble. Then dock in front of the great Temples of Ramses II and Nefertari (one of the great wonders of the world).

Have an unbelievable wedding in King Mena's Palace. The Mena House is a palatial estate that is located at the foot of the Giza Pyramids in Cairo. Your wedding setting includes a Palace with acres and acres of manicured lawn and an Olympic size swimming pool.

The pool is surrounded with white chaises, covered with yellow and white towels, with tall swaying palm trees and erect waiters to attend to your every need.

Brazil

A wedding at New Years in Rio, where everyone dresses in white for the "Yemanja Goddess and Umbanda Cult," celebration and takes their offerings of white flowers into the ocean for prosperity.

Take the cable car to the top of the world to Sugar Loaf and Corcovado for a memorable wedding and view.

Fiji Islands

A romantic Blue Lagoon Cruise in the South Pacific. Visit many of the three hundred islands and share the time of your life in and out of the turquoise waters.

Ecuador, South America

If you are looking for an adventure wedding or honeymoon, try the Amazon Basin in Ecuador. There are several ecological lodges for a romantic experience. Imagine sleeping in a lodge, with an unlocked door. And traveling down the Amazon basin, while bird watching and sighting other creatures.

Cruise on the Explorer II around the Galapagos Islands, to see the natural habitat of sea lions, boobies and other assorted creatures. When you retire to your ship, all the luxury you ever imagined will be waiting for you.

Any Caribbean Island

What is more romantic than a white sand beach with white diamond swells and turquoise water? And of course, there is a private cottage waiting for you, directly on the beach.

How to make your honeymoon sweet:

▼ Discuss your interest and hobby differences. One shouldn't have to sit in the hotel room while the other has all the fun. Find a mutual ground that both can enjoy.

▼ Decide on how much money you want to spend before deciding on your holiday. Have as big a splurge as you can afford without starting your marriage in a financial hole. The best way to do this is to save up – keeping your credit cards for emergencies. You should stay in good hotels and share terrific food. A disappointment on a honeymoon will stay in your memory a lot longer than a dud on any other trip.

Get help to pay for your trip:

Many couples receive a lot of wedding gifts they can't use. Work with a travel agent or tour operator to create a "honeymoon registry" where friends and family can buy you a night in a hotel, a dinner, or a day's worth of rental car or money for shopping. The Artisan Craft Markets are a perfect place to spend some of that money. Make sure to have items in all price ranges—not everyone can afford $150.00.

People love honeymooners.

Let everyone know that you are honeymooners. When booking, ask if there is a honeymoon special price. Even if there aren't, let hotel managers, resort directors, rental-car clerks and waiters know you're on your special trip. You're more likely to get a room upgrade, a nicer car or a bottle of wine. Travel-industry types know that most honeymooners who have a good time will return to re-kindle special memories.

You may have dreamed all your life of your honeymoon, but that doesn't mean it is going to be perfect. Expect the usual glitches and hassles of travel and don't let them ruin or cloud this special time. There can be glitches even when your wedding is on "home turf."

Chapter 12
Most Frequently Asked
Travel Questions

Will I see animals in Africa?

Yes, if you go to a game reserve in Kenya, Tanzania or South Africa.

Are there any skyscrapers in Africa?

The Portuguese, French and British colonized many countries in Africa, but after African independence, they developed modern cosmopolitan cities with skyscrapers.

What is Dakar, Senegal like?

Dakar, Senegal is the capital and it's modern, with deluxe hotels, where you might think you're in the Caribbean. The people lead very sophisticated lives.

Are the streets paved?

The streets are paved in the cities, but not in the villages.

Where can I exchange my money?

At a local bank when you arrive. The only drawback is that you have to fill out papers, show passport and wait in long, long lines, which is a waste of valuable time. I suggest exchanging your money at your hotel, perhaps $100.00 U.S. at a time. When it becomes depleted, you can replace it with another exchange. Money orders and credit cards are widely accepted in the hotels.

How do I tip for service?

Before you depart for your trip, go to your bank and collect $50.00 to $100.00 in single dollar bills to use as tips. Dollars are what Americans understand and there is no confusion regarding the exchange or change.

How many pounds of baggage am I allowed?

You're allowed two bags weighing seventy pounds each and a carry on that must fit in the overhead compartment.

How much purchased goods can I return with?

US customs allows you $450.00 in purchases before imposing a duty tax.

What do I do if I get diarrhea?

Take a swallow of Pepto-Bismol each morning before breakfast to line your stomach. If diarrhea occurs, take a mid laxative early evening and by next morning all signs of diarrhea should disappear.

Can I drink the water?

I suggest you buy bottled water in the hotel or at a local store. It's inexpensive, but would be well worth the investment even if it's costly.

What kind of clothing should I bring to Africa?

Bring 100% cotton T-shirts, jeans, khaki's, casual clothing and good walking shoes.

Can I trade American made items in the market?

Bring lots of T-shirts, sneakers, sunglasses, calculators, walkman, caps, jeans and watches.

Do I need a Visa for Senegal?

No tourist visa is required for entry or exit.

Do I need a yellow fever, shot for Senegal?

No, but if you plan visiting other countries in Africa, I suggest you get a yellow fever shot. The shot is good for ten years.

Should I get a hepatitis shot?

Check with the U.S. Department of Health or the Consulate for the desired country or ask your doctor for inoculation requirements of your desired destination.

Should I take Malaria (Lariam) Pills? How do I take them?

Yes, the health department suggests taking one pill per week starting two weeks before departure and repeat taking the pill for eight consecutive weeks. The substitute for Lariam is Daraprim. Both are prescribed medications.

How much does the Lariam or Daraprim cost?

The Lariam cost approximately $10.00 per pill and the Daraprim cost approximately $1.15 per pill.

Does my insurance cover the cost of the pills and shots?

You must check with your carrier to confirm your coverage.

Do I need a Visa for Egypt?

Yes, you need a visa and you can obtain it from the Egyptian Consulate at 1110 Second Ave., New York City, NY 10022; telephone: 212-759-7120 or contact: Embassy of the Arab Republic of Egypt, 3521 International Court NW, Washington, DC 20008, phone: 202-895-5400 or fax: 202-828-9167

How much is a Visa to Egypt?

The Egypt Visa costs approximately $15.00 US. It's best to check with consulate for exact price. Bring or send two recent photos and valid passport. You can request an application to be mailed to you or pick one up at the consulate.

Can I drink the water in Egypt or Senegal?

I recommend purchasing bottled water from the hotel or at a local store.

What's the capital of Egypt?

Cairo

What is the currency used in Egypt?

The Egyptian pound. Approximately 345 pounds equal one American dollar. The Egyptian pound fluctuates daily.

Can I haggle in the markets in Egypt?

You betcha! Never settle for the first price.

What is the flight time from JFK to Cairo?

Ten hours direct to Cairo

What language do the Egyptians speak?

Arabic and English

What is the religion of the Egyptian majority?

Muslim

Can we organize a group and have a tour designed just for us?

Yes, often special tours are designed for groups.

What is the capacity of a cruise ship on the Nile?

Generally speaking, 150 persons is the limit

How long does it take to cruise from Luxor to Aswan?

The cruise is four nights/five days, with all meals included. It's such a pleasurable tour, that you arrive before you know it.

Can I wear perfume?

I don't suggest wearing perfume because mosquitoes are attracted to the sweet scent.

Do I need to cover up my body in a Muslim country?

Don't expose your body in a suggestive manner. Just be mindful and respectful of their religion.

Are hotels safe?

Yes, hotels are safe. A four star hotel is very safe, but you should place all of your valuables; passport, airline ticket, charge cards, money and anything else that you value in a safe. It leaves you with less to worry about.

Should I bring jewelry?

You may bring your special ornaments, but hopefully they are faux jewelry. Don't flash real jewelry such as diamonds and gold.

How much pocket money should I bring?

I suggest $100.00 per day, which should include some shopping. Americans are known as great shoppers and the locals can spot you a mile away. Naturally the vendors will try to squeeze for your last dime. Be cautious; learn to bargain for the best price.

Where do I get a passport?

You can apply at your local post office or the Passport Office at 376 Hudson St., New York City, NY 10013. However you will need to make an appointment. Please bring two recent passport photos and birth certificate or drivers' license.

Or use the Internet: www.travel.state.gov/passport_service.hml

You can download the passport form from your computer. For regular delivery allow three weeks.

Is there a protection against mosquitoes?

I suggest using Avon Skin So Soft. Apply according to instructions on the bottle.

Can I get an upgrade from coach when traveling with a group?

Yes, you can get an upgrade for an additional cost or if you have frequent flyer miles. However, if you're concerned about leg-room, and want to save money, then ask for a bulkhead or an exit row seat. The bulkhead is the first seat behind the first class or business section. It will give you lots of leg-room for your comfort.

Do I bring bottled water with me?

Don't bring water with you, because you can easily purchase bottled water when you arrive at your destination. It's fairly inexpensive.

What shots do I need for the destination that I am traveling to?

Please check with the Immigration Department or the Consulate of the country you are traveling to for inoculation information.

What do I wear when visiting a tropical destination?

You should wear lots of 100% cotton clothing items and comfortable shoes for touring. I don't suggest new shoes, because they can wear on your feet and cause blisters.

Where do I find out whether I need a Visa or a shot for my journey?

Please check with your travel agency or on the Internet. Locate the Consulate for that country in this book, and call them. They will be able to provide you with all the vital travel information.

What is the temperature for the destination where I am traveling?

Call your local Consulate or Tourist Board for the average temperature for the time of year you are traveling. You can also log on to their web-site for updated information.

What is the time difference between my destination?

Check with your travel agent or refer to the Internet or newspaper for the time change.

Is my hotel centrally located?

You want to be centrally located to save time on your holiday. Always check with your travel agent and do a little research to determine the distance from hotel to most of your activities.

Is it safe to bathe in the bath water?

It is always safe to bathe at your hotel, as long as you don't swallow it.

What kind of hotel am I staying in?

Always ask for a four star hotel. Because each country's standards are different, you don't want to be relegated to less than what you expect. It's better to pay a little more and get what you expect than to be surprised at sub-standard accommodations. Most Americans want the comforts of home when they travel.

What's the difference between a Passport and a Visa?

Your country issues a Passport as a form of identification. The passport is your proof of citizenship of the country you claim. And it allows you permission to exit and enter your country. The turn around time for a new or renewed passport is approximately three weeks from the day you apply.

The country that you are visiting issues a Visa. A Visa allows you permission to enter and exit their country. There is a nominal cost for a Visa that is paid to the consulate of the country you desire to visit. Check with your travel agent or the local consulate for your desired destination. You can also explore the Internet for more information regarding Visas.

What kind of insurance do I get when I charge my ticket on my credit card?

American Express offers $100,000.00 for life and accident insurance and Global Assist® will locate an international hospital or doctor for you.

MasterCard suggests you check with your bank of issuance for specific details regarding your card. They offer pre-trip information such as an advisory on weather, local currency and local immunization. It's best to call your MasterCard Bank to inquire about their insurance policies.

Visa Gold or Platinum Card offers $150,000.00 in life and travel accident insurance. For lost baggage, they will help in finding assistance to locate your baggage. And they will suggest medical locations in foreign countries. For the Classic card, there is no insurance, but they will assist with lost or stolen cards and block further usage of stolen cards. You have to pay separately for travel insurance.

You can obtain a comprehensive travel protection plan insurance from your travel agent. Your travel insurance covers: trip cancellation/interruption protection, emergency medical, dental coverage, emergency medical transportation, baggage coverage, baggage delay, vacation delay, travel accident, trip inconvenience, collision/loss damage benefit (optional) and 24-hour hotline assistance. However the maximum amount of trip cancellation/interruption coverage is $20,000.00.

Is it safe to travel with children?

I think children should be exposed to the different cultures around the world, the earlier, the better. Taking young children along will give them a better understanding of other people and it allows them to open their eyes and accept other cultures. I have hosted many trips where parents have brought along their children. The children have shared the best time meeting children from other countries.

How do I locate the Consulate for my desired destination?

Ask your travel agent or search the web for the Consulate of the country that you desire to visit. Usually consulates are located in major cities throughout the United States. See page xx for a list of Consulates and Embassies.

When is the best time to go to West Africa?

The month of February is Black History Month and it's an excellent time to visit the Motherland and learn about our history.

What is the temperature in Brazil during the months of November to February?

It's the summer season and you'd better bring your sun-block because it's hot, hot, hot! The temperature averages 95 degrees. After all, you are going to the opposite side of the Equator.

What should I expect in Fiji?

First, lots of sunshine and friendly people. Because Fiji is located in the South Pacific, the weather is warm year round. Seventy-five percent of the people are of African descent. There are 300 islands available to cruise to. You might want to visit a local village where they will invite you in to share a bowl of Kava. Kava is a local native drink that looks like mud and tastes the same. It's supposed to relax you.

How many hours does it take to arrive in Fiji from New York City?

It takes five and a half-hours from JFK or Newark on United Airlines to arrive in Los Angeles and ten hours non-stop on Pacific Airways to Fiji. The stop over in Los Angeles is approximately 3-½ hours. So the total number of hours is nineteen. But what a wonderful place to feast your eyes!

Can you recommend a destination for a honeymoon?

Fiji is on top of my list, because it's relaxing and takes the stress away from your relationship. On the many islands of Fiji all you have to do is lay back, be pampered and enjoy. There is lots of aquamarine Pacific Ocean water with white diamond swells rushing to the shore.

I'm thinking of a destination to ski. Where would you suggest?

I would suggest Austria. There is nothing like the snow-capped mountains and slopes of Austria. Plus the towns are filled with lots of history, tradition and culture.

What local destination would you suggest I visit for Carnival?

If you want a domestic Carnival, I would suggest New Orleans. It's one of our most Southern cities and is filled with treasures. Mardi Gras is not the only find when you visit New Orleans; this is a party town year-round, especially in the French Quarter. But if you choose to venture a little further south, try a Carnival in one of the Caribbean Island such as Trinidad or Barbados. But there's no Carnival like a Brazilian Carnival, especially in Bahia and Rio. The world knows of their Carnival, they spare no bars.

What's the best airline to take to Brazil?

Varig, United, JAL, TAM. They are all respectable airlines, so you have your choice.

Is it true that Salvador do Bahia, Brazil has the largest African population outside of Africa?

Yes, it's not only true, but it's a beautiful experience to see our brothers and sisters greet us as we arrive in their Portuguese speaking country. The Brazilians are so alive with energy and a zest for living.

Now that you know how to get ready for the trip, here are some of the sights you'll see.

Part 2
The Places

Ivory Coast

Women and girls carrying provisions on their heads

Merchant with fabric on his head in village up the lagoon of the Ivory Coast

Chapter 1
Ivory Coast: Black and Proud

The African Continent is larger than life. It's five times the size of the United States. I first visited the city of Abidjan in the Ivory Coast. As the plane landed, all kinds of thoughts flashed through my mind. I had no idea of what to expect or what I'd see. As I stepped out of the plane, I saw a cluster of the most magnificent, elegant, tall, ebony colored people with clear, clean complexions and warm, welcoming smiles. They look similar to many of my relatives here in the States or other African American walking down the streets in New York City. The only difference was that the men were dressed in African Boubous (African attire). Women wore lots of colorful printed African cotton or Kente cloth wrapped and draped around their waist and over their shoulders carrying their babies tucked on their backs while balancing baskets of household provisions on their head. They sashayed along the roads with a very erect posture. The tropical temperature inspired me to dress casual as the locals do.

The Ivory Coast had been a French Colony for two hundred years, and then became independent in 1963. Although still influenced by the French, it has developed two distinct cultures, African (knowing where they came from) and French (where they had been). The city of Abidjan is very cosmopolitan with skyscrapers, mainly built after its independence.

I stayed in the tower annex of the Hotel I'voire, located in Cocody along the lagoon. Just beyond my panoramic view, I saw Le Plateau, which is the commercial business section with skyscrapers. Across the lagoon I viewed the simplicity of a fishermen's village.

Cocody is an affluent residential area with luxury hotels, homes of diplomats and wonderful Chic Cafe's with an eclectic group of friendly locals. My evening thirst was quenched with Mamba Beer accompanied by French fries, all under the stars of a clear, African sky. I also heard Latin music from a distant bistro. "Life is good," I said to myself. This is how I see Africa. I always take a little time to relax and exchange conversation with the locals. I want to find out about their dreams, aspirations and culture.

There was "Africaness" all around me. I knew I was home. As I traveled into town, there was more "Africaness" in the hotels, banks, markets, businesses etc. It was a wonderful feeling. Now, I understand what James Brown meant when he sang "Black & Proud."

I visited several villages across the lagoon and brought hard candies and pens for the children. The villages appeared to be lost in a time warp. Some of the women bared their breasts, but not in the cosmopolitan city of Abidjan. African men of the Muslim religion can have as many wives as they can support. Eighty percent of the country is Muslim and during the month of February, Ramenden is celebrated. They fast from food, drinks and sex from dawn to dusk.

While touring the city of Abidjan, I stopped at the Rive Banco where men were washing clothes against a rubber tire anchored by a rock. Their long, lean, muscular bodies gyrated with an up and down motion to the silent rhythm of the African drum.

Shopping in the Treichville market can be an artful adventure or a scary experience. All the merchants approached me at once to sell their wares. But I was not interested in buying anything on the first visit. One vendor called me, "Uncle Jim." An American whispered through her teeth, "I think he means Uncle Tom." The merchants hawked and followed me, referring to me as "Brother, brother, brother." It was very annoying and an approach I wasn't familiar with. Another vendor announced, "You are my friend," but after his repeated persistence I replied, "I'm your best friend." "No, you no my friend; you no buy nothing," he responded.

Traveling down to the Grand Bassam, which is a coastal town along a stretch of beach, I saw artisan shops, museums, and grand mansions in disrepair and swaying palm trees lining the long winding lonely paved roads. The palm trees also hover over the thatched roof restaurant where I lunched on fresh fish, the catch of the day.

At the turn of the century the French built mansions and died shortly after contracting yellow fever. Their mansions still stand to remind us of their lavish life style. At a cocktail party at the Mayor's house, I suggested restoring and converting the Grand Bassam into a luxury resort to attract tourism.

The bus ride from Abidjan to Yamoussoukro takes a half-day, but it's worth it. The Basilica is so massive, as we approached the town I could see the grand dome rising over the city from a distance. It stands out like a sore thumb. It's the largest Basilica outside of Rome. The Basilica expands over 148 acres where once rubber trees stood. The late President Felix Houphouet-Boigny, built it as a monument to himself. Unfortunately, the only visitors to the Basilica are tourists, because ninety percent of the country is Muslim. I was puzzled to see all white saints in the stained glass windows. Just behind the Basilica is a mansion that was built as a guesthouse for the Pope's brief three-day visit.

The university and many government buildings were constructed after their independence. Just in front of the president's residence is a pond with a collection of crocodiles that cast a watchful eye on the palace. I returned to the States focused with a new center and proud of my heritage. I had discovered one of the fifty-three African countries.

Senegal

Woman in market

Pink Lake, Senegal

Above: Fishermen's boats on shore

Left: Local waiting for the ferry to Goree Island.

Chapter 2
Dakar, Senegal: The Motherland

The moment I entered the Air Afrique plane at JFK, I began to feel 'The Motherland.' It was an unbelievable experience to see Black pilots, flight attendants and so many Black people in general.

While flying over the same water that our forefathers were once forced to tread, I looked through my window and thought of how our forefathers and mothers were captured and had suffered unmentionable atrocities for 350 years. Their means of transport was totally different from my experience. Back then, a ship took them months to cross the Atlantic Ocean.

Visiting the motherland was a culture shock and enlightening experience. Dakar, Senegal in West Africa is the closest point to the United States and it was a good starting point. After a 7½ hour non-stop flight we landed in Leopold Senghor Airport, named after their first president and famous poet. Senegal had been colonized by France but received its independence in 1960. The population is nine million people.

When we arrived, the tropical temperature inspired me to dress casually as the locals do. Men wore long flowing grand boubous of rich earth tones and the women dress in beautiful African printed cotton cloth. Women generally draped fabric around their hips and shoulders and wrap their heads with a twist of matching cloth. "Welcome brothers and sisters," and *"Nanga.def"* (how are you), the locals cheerfully called out, I responded, *"Mangi rek"* (I am fine). I knew I was home.

Although French and Wolof is the local language, English is widely spoken in the business world. The CFA is the currency. At this writing 590 CFA's equals approximately one U.S. dollar.

Mohammed, our guide met and transferred us to my favorite hotel, the Savanna. The Savanna is perched on the side of a hill. The accommodations are located several steps down from the street level through a lush garden of flowers and greenery with several standing, painted, wooden statues of Colonized figures. Each room had large picture windows facing the Atlantic Ocean. Each morning I shared a buffet breakfast of croissants, omelets, fresh squeezed juices, yogurt and fresh fruit on the verandah overlooking a 300-foot pool that was surrounded by white chaise and wind blown swaying palm trees. At the opposite end of the hotel was an enormous restaurant suspended over the Atlantic Ocean, a perfect spot for a romantic encounter. The hotel also had a boutique, tennis court, spa and deck to anchor your boat and another to sunbathe and watch the time go by. I walked out on the dock early one morning and sat under the gazebo to reflex on my visit to Senegal. Just a short distance across the bay, I saw Goree Island rising out of the sea and I pondered over its turbulent past.

Dakar is the capital city of Senegal, it's also the pulse of the nation with skyscrapers and many squares that have been dedicated to many world leaders. Independence Square is in the center of town and a few steps from everything one would need to do or see. There are fast food restaurants, boutiques and nightclubs on Avenue de Pompidou (a main boulevard). Dakar also has a gambling casino and several discos to dance the night away.

There are many things and places to explore during your visit. I recommend the IFAN museum on Mandela Square. It houses one of the best collections of artifacts: fetish mask, musical instruments and ceremonial costumes from Benin, Ivory Coast, Guinea, Mali, Ghana, Senegal, Mauritania, Nigeria and many other West African countries. I was a bit surprised when the guide permitted me to touch the exhibit on display. Upon my exit, I purchased a coffee table book of photos of the exhibition so I could savor every moment of my personalized tour.

My city tour included a spin around Independent Square, a visit to a mosque, a craft market and a stop at the gate in front of the President's Palace, which was a large white palace in the heart of the city. I took a photo opportunity with a uniformed guard who keeps a watchful eye on the palace.

No visit is complete without shopping in the markets: Soumedioune Market is located along the cornice lining the Atlantic Ocean. It's comprised of a cluster of vendors in an open-air market where you must negotiate. It's a popular spot for tourists. There are lots of vendors anxious to sell their woodcarvings, statues, gold jewelry and leather and skin goods and batiks. Each batik tells a story of a harvest or the daily life of a village. Across the street from the market is a collection of shops with antique carvings, in various sizes, and hand carved wood furniture on display.

Just north of Soumedioune on the shore is a daily fish market. Fishermen return to shore in their colorful dugouts, just before the sun goes down. They transport their catch of the day which consists of a variety of fish that women, children and men prepare to sell. I raced along the shore to capture the moment. Fishing is a tradition along the Atlantic coast and seafood is the basic staple of their diet.

The Sandango Market is in the center of town and it's really the essence of Dakar because of its energy and aggressive salesmen and women. Everyone comes out of their stall to greet and sell cotton quilted printed bags, shirts, boubous, shoes, beads, mudcloth, cameras etc. You have to spend time negotiating and bargaining. It's part of their culture. One of my favorite markets is the Camel, because they have a variety of colorful woven baskets in different sizes. I purchased one to use as a hamper. Of course they sell woodcarvings and masks—some look like authentic antiques. The food market is near the Goree Island Ferry terminal, where they sell fresh fruit, fish, meat, cocoa butter, etc.

Most of the merchants are interested in trading American items, so bring lots of T-shirts, baseball caps, sneakers, calculators, sun glasses, tote bags, watches, jeans, shoes etc., be prepared to bargain hard and long. As we walked through the streets, suddenly we were met and surrounded by a parade of people selling their wares; women selling dolls from a basket on their head; men carrying masks and other hand crafted items and a bundle of cotton printed pants, etc.

There are so many sights to explore in the city. The Church of Saviour is unusual, because black saints are painted on the ceiling and along the walls, while white saints are in the stain glass windows. The guide explained that the church is for everyone. There are lots of mosques throughout the city because the majority of the population is Muslim.

The city of Dakar doesn't have any building codes, so everyone builds as they like. I saw a shack next to an architecturally beautifully designed home. Most of the homes are constructed from cinder block and covered with plaster, then painted in shades of pastel.

Tucked away in an alley was my favorite factory that's open twenty-four hours a day. I always venture down those dark streets in the middle of the night to find assorted size cloth purses, bags, talking drum covers, shirts, pants, mud-cloth jackets, etc at half the market price. It's worth the trip. Always travel with a companion and take a taxi in the evening. Negotiate your round-trip price before you get in the taxi and ask him to wait for your return trip.

I always treat people with kindness and respect and end up getting a lot in return. I talk with locals and make friends; they have helped me find special places that only the locals know about and tourists would envy.

I think one of the most romantic dinner spots is Lagune 11 Restaurant. It's a theme restaurant with a nautical interior. The restaurant jets out on a pier into the Atlantic Ocean overlooking Goree Island. Yousson N'Dour, a popular African singer, has planted his roots in Dakar with a popular nightclub where he entertains on weekends. He has also built a clubhouse music studio at a cost of $300,000.00 U.S.

One of my favorite nightspots is Ponti, a jazz/blues restaurant bar where an eclectic group of locals hang out nightly. The band played James Brown's "Black and Proud". I grabbed someone's jacket and threw it around the singers shoulder, a la James Brown. Later, I asked a fellow traveler if she wanted to dance; she quickly extended her right arm and threw her head back with a dramatic tango gesture. Dakar also has a gambling casino and several discos to dance the night away.

While walking down the streets, I witnessed men holding hands. At first I thought it was a sexual thing. One afternoon, our guide grabbed my hand; I reacted uncomfortably for a few moments. Then I realized that he was complimenting me, by holding my hand. It's a sign of friendship in West Africa. Our guide informed me that it's their custom. The wonderful thing about traveling around the world is that I have been introduced to many cultures and have become enlightened to how the rest of the world lives and accepts different gestures.

Goree Island is a main tourist attraction. We boarded a ferry for a twenty-minute ride across the bay. The ferry was filled with an eclectic group of locals, wearing traditional boubous, transporting their wares and food, all mixed with a collection of gawking tourists. Someone yelled out, "What kind of shit is this?"

As we approached Goree Island, the pastel, dusty rose colored houses appeared mysteriously through a haze. During the disembarkation from the ferry I walked along the cornice to the Museum of History. As I entered one of several rooms depicting the slave trade, my mouth dropped and I stopped, disbelieving, the sight of skeletons of our ancestors buried together in a large block of cement, their mouths open, their skulls crying out from the pain they had suffered. The skeletons graphically displayed elements of torture; I could hear their loud cries and I was reduced to tears.

The highlight of the tour was at the House of the Slaves; Dr. Joseph Ndiaye lectured on the conditions and existence of the slave trade. He informed us that the Portuguese, Spaniards, Dutch and the English perpetuated the trade within the four walls of the house. He was emphatic and outraged regarding the comparison of the Holocaust that existed for only eleven years to three hundred and fifty years of slavery. "Nobody every talks about slavery. We need to be reminded, so this catastrophe never happens again. 'Roots' was only the tip of the iceberg." He firmly stated. He demonstrated how slaves where captured then shackled with chains around their waists and wrists. He also showed how their ankles were attached to an iron ball and chain, totally preventing them from escaping. If a slave was defiant, he was forced into a 4 x 4 compartment with twenty-men cramped under the stairwell to lay in feces and urine. There was a tiny opening in the wall to allow a bit of daylight. Men were only allowed out once a day to stretch. The rebellious men were beaten and thrown into the Atlantic Ocean to be eaten by sharks. The iron ball prevented them from escaping the inevitable.

Many young ladies indulged in sexual favors with the slave traders who lived upstairs over the slave quarters in order to become pregnant. Once impregnated, they were set free. After the lecture, Dr. Ndiaye autographed and sold copies of the History of Goree Island book.

Moments later, everyone gathered downstairs at the 'Door of No Return'. The door opens on to the Atlantic Ocean. It's called the 'Door of no

Return' because once the captives passed through, they were shipped to the Americas or the Caribbean, never to return. Everyone joined hands, formed a circle and took a moment to reflect and remember in silence. "We must never forget what happened here and never allow it to happen again," stated Dr. Ndiaye. Everyone was asked to call out the name of the person who inspired him or her.

One of the travelers walked on the rocks along the shore and tossed the ashes of her late husband into the ocean. "I promised him that someday we'd go to Africa. I felt a sense of peace within myself after tossing the ashes. We did make that journey," she told us. There wasn't a dry eye in the house.

After everyone dried his or her eyes, the journey continued to a primary school. The director was a very stately gentleman with charming manners. The staircase leading to the second floor was embraced and intertwined with colorful bougainvillea. The director wore a grand boubou (three-piece long flowing boubou with a tunic and pants). He told us if he knew we were coming, he would have arranged to have the children meet us in the courtyard. After exchanging polite conversation, I presented him with four boxes of new books.

As I entered a classroom, I yelled "Bonjour, les enfants," and they responded, "Bonjour, Monsieur." They stood and sang a beautiful tribute to us. It was such an uplifting experience; I began handing out Bic pens, pencils and paper to the children. Their faces lit up as if I had handed them a pot of gold. The female professors were beautifully dressed in colorful African boubous. After departing from the school we toured another craft market and a lonely Catholic Church. The church is lonely because most of the country is Muslim.

After the short tour, I sat at a table in an outdoor café overlooking the beach to reflect on the morning's total experience. The table was shaded with a large parasol to protect me from the burning sun under a clear blue sky. I ordered a flag beer to compliment my typical Senegal dish of fresh fish and rice with salad. I loved hearing the rushing sound of the waves splashing against the shore and children playing nearby. I thought, how lucky these children are not to have been born 150 years ago, but how blessed they are to have gained a future.

Goree Island was an exhilarating, educational, historical, emotional and memorable experience that should be shared with family and friends.

Just outside of the city of Dakar is one of Senegal's miracles, Pink Lake, where the water really is pink. Pink Lake became a tourist attraction in 1985 and continues to draw the curious. As the sun reflects on the minerals at the bottom of the lake, the water appears pink. But when the sun doesn't shine, the water is aubergine. After arriving at the lake we boarded a four-wheel drive that taxied us directly to the shore. I observed men mining salt from the bottom of the lake and tossing it in their dugout boats. Women walked deep into the salty water with colorful plastic pails and collected brown, gray and pink salt from the boats. They lifted and balanced the pails on their heads and carried them ashore and placed them carefully in cone shapes on the shore. The hot sun dried and bleached the salt so that it could be bagged and shipped for commercial consumption. The lake is constantly mined, so they have to rotate the location so that the salt gets a chance to replenish its natural balance and growth. Pink Lake is one of Gods miracles.

After the salt dried on their bodies, it turned white andit appeared as tie-dyed ringlets of zigzag configurations on their ebony skin. Actually at first glance I thought they were wearing tie-dyed T-shirts. Everyone was slim, fit and salty. I dipped my feet in the water and they instantly became white. The concentration of salt was so strong that I found it difficult to understand how the Senegalese people could withstand it. But it's a way to earn a salary.

Children from the near by villages suddenly appeared offering bottles of artfully arranged colorful salt, the bottles looked as if they had been painted from the inside. Women carried African dolls in baskets on their heads and young men carried woodcarvings for sale.

After a walk along the lake, we boarded our four-wheel drive and chugged over hills of desert sand that took us to a Fulani Village. I felt as if I had been on a roller coaster. A crop of dunes on the beach isolated the village. There were many thatched roof huts for the extended family. Several members of the village guided us around and introduced us to their culture. One of the huts was used as a kitchen where food was cooked daily over a wood burning flame. Another hut had neatly arranged furniture and the dirt floors had been swept with a broom. Several guests sat on the bed and observed and learned about the daily life in the village.

I observed a young lady in the yard standing over at the water well. She dropped a colorful plastic bucket attached to a rope into the well to retrieve water. We could not drink from the well because our bodies are not conditioned to the bacteria. I suggest buying bottled water in the stores before taking an excursion. The weather is very dry and water is the only way to satisfy the thirst.

Women carried their babies on their backs wrapped in colorful printed fabric that was twisted and draped around their bodies. Babies are transported wherever the mother goes. Often the baby continues to sleep while the mother bends in an up and downward motion. I watched a baby bob on the back of his mother while she was beating grain with a maillot in a large wooden bowl.

The village was filled with lots of dusty children who had been playing in the sand. Many children requested Bic pens for school. They are quite used to visiting tourists and welcome them with open arms. There were several thatched roof huts for the extended family. The family is very important in Africa. Several generations live together and support each other spiritually and financially.

We re-boarded our four-wheel for a short ride over the roller coaster dunes to an incredibly, clean, long, lonely stretch of lush beach where the balmy, turquoise, aqua marine water with white diamond swells thrashed against white powered beach sand.

After our photo opportunity, we boarded and headed through the sand dunes for lunch at a restaurant under a thatched roof. At the entrance was a man playing a Kora—a typical Senegalese string musical instrument. It looks like a large banjo. I believe the base is constructed from a very large calabash. The singing musician walked from table to table including the names of the guests in the song. Of course we were requested to tip him. The thatched roof reminded me that I was in Africa, sharing the many personalities of the country. "This was Africa."

A short drive away is the island of Joal Fadiouth, where the first President, Mr. Leopold Sengore was born. I had invited my mother to share Senegal with me. As we traveled south passing many baobab trees and open

Savanna, we passed several small towns and villages where the residents gleefully smiled and waved us pass.

When we arrived on the shore of Joal Fadiouth, we were extremely thirsty because the temperature was hot. So I raced into a thatched roof store to purchase several large bottles of Flag beer to quench our thirst. Just ahead of us was a long, long weather beaten wooden planked bridge that connected us to the other side of the island. We were cautioned to watch our step because over a period of time some of the planks had become weather beaten and misplaced.

As we slowly crossed the bridge, we observed a collection of huts standing erect, supported by stilts raising five feet from the water. The only means of transportation to those thatched roof huts was a paddle and a dugout. The dugouts are painstakingly handcrafted from large logs.

After a long, long walk across the bridge, we arrived at the village. The streets, the houses and shops are totally constructed from seashells and cement. I don't know what it is about children, but I think they are special and adorable. We were greeted with lots of warm smiles and a curious, "Where are you from?" This was not the end of our little walking tour. Around the corner at the back of the island was another long bridge that landed us in a graveyard where the coffins were raised above the ground. My mother was exhausted from the schlepp, she sat on the end of a tomb. The guide informed her that it wasn't polite to sit on a tomb. "It won't hurt him, because I'm sitting on his feet," she responded.

Later we browsed the market—there is always a market in every village. Lucky me, I found another market to spend my last dime. I selected some trinkets for several friends. We were invited into a thatched roof shell hut to view their tradition and culture. There was no gas or electric stove, fire was made from burning wood in a separate hut, which they refer to as the kitchen. Water was retrieved from the well or large container collected the rain. There are no carpets, just dirt floors, with simple furnishings, like a bed or mat to sleep on.

Another day we visited Saly, a luxury resort, consisting of five four star hotels that are located directly on an open beachfront stretch of the Atlantic Ocean. We stayed at the Savanna. It's a spacious, well appointed resort with lots of amenities such as an Olympic size pool, poolside bar, craft markets, swaying palm trees etc. All of the properties offer some of the same amenities and activities—it's always lots of fun to compare. On the grounds of the Savanna there are a collection of thatched roof huts with modern plumbing. The huts reminded me that I was still in Africa.

Whenever I travel, I always carry my bathing trunks, just in case I see a pool. I dash into the changing room before lunch to take a dip in the pool. While doing the backstroke and a flip, I heard salsa music ringing from the rafters. I decided to do another back flip before joining the dance lesson. The salsa movement is all in the hips and I knew exactly what to do. As I swiveled my hips, the instructor asked if I was from New York because I danced so well.

After a little work out, I walked along the long wooden planked pier to get a broader perspective of the coastline. There was a young man fishing on the pier and he offered me his line so that I could catch a fish. I thanked him and told him that I would rather observe the scenery. Then I clicked my little Mickey Mouse camera with a panoramic view to capture the moment. I thought I had died and gone to heaven because the environment was so peaceful, without a soul to disturb me. I walked for miles along the beach and almost forgot about lunch.

When I finally returned from my excursion, everyone was noshing away. I ordered the typical Senegalese dish, a whole fish on a bed of rice with an onion sauce and several cold bottles of Flag beer, then a bottle of cold Fanta. Flag is different from American beer; it's light and very pleasant going down.

Sine Saloum is also south of Dakar. I slept most of the journey because I suffer from motion sickness. After a long drive passing many villages where enterprising entrepreneurs created markets selling a variety of condiments, souvenirs and cotton printed African cloth we arrived in Saloum. Saloum is comprised of hinterland which is the groundnut (peanut) growing basin of Senegal and the Saloum Delta, a myriad of small islands scattered between innumerable channels.

Perched on the shore of Saloum is the Pelican hotel, which is comprised of several thatched roof huts, a large swimming pool and an open-air dining room. After refreshing our faces, we walked to the shore and boarded a dugout to motor through the mangroves where we saw oysters attached to the roots of the trees. Saloum is also a paradise for bird watchers. I watched pelicans spread their winds, marabou storks, pink flamingos, egrets, eagles and black belly birds, etc. I also saw an assortment of birds resting on branches or white sand barges while observing our passage. There are no alligators because they can't survive in salt water.

Saloum Delta is comprised of 300,000 acres of unspoiled mangrove. I dipped my hands in the water, they turned white after the salt dried. Several young men maneuvered and guided our colorful, painted dugout (boat) through the mangrove. As we traveled through the mangrove, I didn't see another person or village in sight. I wondered if we'd ever return for lunch.

As we continued our journey, I observed the horizon from the river's edge. The earth formed a circumference around us that drifted into the sky. For a moment, it appeared that the only thing that existed were a few boats and several baobab trees. A baobab tree appears as if its turned downside up because the branches look like roots reaching for the sky. It's the logo of Senegal. From a distance I witnessed a lone baobab tree standing on a white sand beach. I was lost in thought in this oasis of tranquility with just the sound of water gently splashing against our boat. While cruising from island to island, I discovered a completely different personality of landscape at every turn. There were borders of white sandy beaches and extremely dense vegetation and small villages where fishermen sheltered beneath coconut palms. I could have just cruised these peaceful waters for hours all the while being inspired to write and breathe in the fresh unspoiled, unpolluted air.

I used my camera to photograph this natural habitat, though I wish I owned a real zoom camera so I could have captured those special moments up close. There was also a lonely baobab tree standing tall on a single small, picturesque island.

When we returned to shore, we were met by a group of young men who assisted us as we disembarked. One of them remembered me from a previous trip. After returning to the Pelican Hotel, we passed several thatched roof huts on our way to the dining room, which is located in the main building. The hotel offers comfortable accommodations overlooking the river. I was extremely thirsty so I sat and quickly devoured two Flag beers before lunch.

Lunch included Tiebujen (fish and rice covered with onions in a tomato paste) and Yassa genar (fish or chicken with rice smothered with onions and lemon juice), complimented with a lettuce and tomato salad and several cold Flag beers. Our table faced the Olympic size pool where Europeans lazed on chaise around the pool. Unfortunately, I didn't have time to share the pool in order to chill. After lunch, we gathered for our return journey to Dakar.

No matter how many times I return to Senegal, it's never the same. There are always nuances that make it a very special place. As I go deeper into their culture I always discover something new. I also open my eyes and my heart and see things a little different each time.

During February's Black History Month Tour, everyone dresses in African Boubous for the farewell dinner and re-naming ceremony and looks very regal, I couldn't distinguish the Africans from African-Americans. It's such a spiritual experience receiving a new African name and a certificate from a high Priest. That's when I really felt my new center.

Gambia

Left: Village life

Below: Lonely beach scene with dugouts and baobab trees

Thatched roof guest houses at Juffureh

Mama TyeDye doing her thing in the yard

Right: View of shore as we depart Banjul, Gambia

Chapter 3
Roots in the Gambia—
A Land Filled with History and Art

I had longed to visit The Gambia, especially after having seen the television melodrama, 'Roots' by Alex Haley. I wanted to connect and discover my roots. I spent several nights in Dakar and opted for an overnight in The Gambia.

The drive to The Gambia is a four-hour long stretch of patched, bumpy paved road, making for an uncomfortable trip. I asked the driver, "Are the pot holes in the road to slow the traffic? They are just holes in the road." he responded. As we passed many small villages and markets, locals were dressed in traditional colorful printed African boubous. The markets had displays of cooking utensils and assorted grain and seasoning laid on colorful fabrics on the ground.

Four hours later we arrived at the Gambia border, where there was a long line of cars and trucks waiting for the custom officials to issue a visa for entry. The cost of the visa had just been raised two days before from $12.00 to $32.00 US. There was no way I could have known in advance. Everyone on the bus started to bitch and moan. "You're in an emerging country, you've just spent thousands of dollars to get here, so what's another few dollars?" I questioned. Everyone suggested that we turn around and drive back to Dakar. "No way, "I shouted. "If twenty dollars means that much to you, you should cut back on your shopping or wait here at the border and we'll pick you up tomorrow." Then suddenly everyone agreed to pay and we proceeded to the dock to wait for a ferry that would bring us across the Banjul River.

The Gambia is a small country located in the stomach of Senegal. English is the national language because once upon a time the British colonized the country. Several other dialects are also spoken, such as Wolof.

While waiting for the ferry, someone asked, "What times does the ferry get here?" "When it gets here," the guide responded. There are only two ferries that alternate crossing every two hours depending on the tide. It's a very slow moving vehicle; it takes approximately forty-five minutes to cross. Once the ferry arrived a huge crush of people, cars, buses, chickens, ox, fish, bicycles, etc all crush into a tight squeeze. The back of our bus was suspended over the end of the ferry, I dare not tell anyone for fear that they would have panicked. A young man approached my window and stated in a very mature voice, "I am a school boy." Initially I found humor in his approach, then reached in my bag and gave him several bic pens for school. As we crossed the calm river, I saw lots of fishermen dugouts and small peaceful villages along the shore. After a short while I ventured out of the bus to explore the deck. One of the passengers stood 6'5" tall. He was very regal, and he looked like a King dressed in a grand golden boubou. From the upper deck, I viewed the harbor from both sides of the river.

After we disembarked in Banjul, the capital city of The Gambia, we boarded a transfer bus to escort us to the Atlantic Beach Hotel. The hotel is a luxury property located on a long stretch of beachfront property. The British built the hotel during the colonization. It has a variety of amenities, such as a large Olympic size pool with lots of chaise, a restaurant next to the pool, a boutique, disco, a bar and a formal dining room. As everyone checked in, I immediately dashed pass the Olympic size swimming pool and chaise lounges under the swaying palm trees where I shared lunch at a table facing the river. I observed young schoolgirls playfully walking along the beach in brightly colored school uniforms; some carried fresh fruit over their head. The temperature was hot. I ordered a cold beer to cool my body and shared a seafood lunch. There is nothing like being located on the river with fresh fish on your plate.

Gambia is a paradise for Europeans because the temperature is hot and mild. Banjul is a quiet town with lots of history. Standing in the heart of town is a monument that commemorates their independence from

Britain. The Gambia also has a national museum that should not be missed. The paved roads that lead through town are lined with small colonial structures to reflect its past. As we traveled through town we saw lots of fine craft markets displaying woodcarvings and batiks. Shopping in The Gambia is less expensive than Senegal and everyone speaks English.

Next stop was at the Alligator farm, where alligators actually float on top of the Lilly pond with just their eyes peeking from the foliage of green leaves covering the pond. I was told these creatures are friendly, although their skin is very cold. I couldn't believe that the guide asked me to pet one. No way! Several people began petting them, not my favorite thing to do. One of those suckers crawled out of the pond and approached me with his mouth open. I did not stick around to find out how friendly he was. I was not interested in becoming his next meal. Instead of waiting, I ran off and went shopping in one of the craft markets to haggle with a vendor over a four-foot wooden statue of a very graceful lady carrying a basket on her head. I negotiated from $250.00 to $50.00 U.S. and clinched the deal. I thought it would be a terrific prop for my television show, "GlobeTrotter Jon Haggins".

While shopping, we entered Mama Tie-Dye's hut, she was lying on a very thin mattress on the floor, wearing a boubou that revealed her breasts from the side. Her pocketbook was strapped on her shoulder. She was watching color television while surrounded by wall-to-wall tie-dyed fabric on racks stacked to the ceiling. Her gray Mercedes was covered with dust and parked in the yard. She also had several clotheslines of tie-dyed fabric and batiks hanging outside and a tall rack stacked with more fabric in front of her door. I asked her if she took traveler's checks?" "Oh, yeah honey. No problem," mama replied.

The stacks of tie-dyed fabric included pants, boubous, tablecloths and napkins and tie-dyed fabrics for you to be creative with. I bargained for a pair of tie-dyed pants for which mama was asking $10.00. She smiled and told me, "You African-American brother, I like you, so you can take the pants for $6.00."

Our evening was filled with live entertainment such as a local fashion show and a band playing African music and sounds. The best part of the evening was a buffet of delicious fresh food and desserts. After dinner, I retired to my grand suite, in my grand bed. What a treat. I slept like a baby with no interruption until the next morning.

We departed early in order to catch the first ferry. I couldn't believe the size of the crowd that had arrived before the break of day. There were cars, jeeps, trucks, buses and passengers waiting at the gate. God knows what time they arrived. We missed the first ferry, but while waiting for the next, several vendors were selling trinkets and batiks, bags and exchanging dollarses (which is the currency, 11 dollars are equal to $1 U.S.). Several tourists exchanged items for merchandise. One girl exchanged her mother's shoes for bracelets, necklaces and T-shirts. During the two-hour or more wait, I exited the bus with Donna, a travel mate, and walked through the gate to check out the shops on the other side of the street. This was an eventful morning.

Finally it was our turn to board the ferry for another river crossing. After our bus disembarked on the opposite side of the river, we headed for Juffereh, home of Alex Haley's ancestors. Along the bumpy road, a woman was walking alone, I asked the driver to stop and offer her a lift. For as far as I could see there was only a savanna of wilderness and open fields, wild grass and baobab trees. It was just too hot, and there wasn't a village in sight. Upon accepting the ride, she told us that her daughter had just given birth to a baby. She was going to share the good news with relatives in the next village. Family is very important in the African culture. Several generations live in the same house and would never consider living elsewhere, because each member of the family is an intricate part of the support system, both spiritually and financially. There is no welfare in the country. Everyone in the family has to work. Grandmothers are available to baby-sit and are helpful with other household duties. Older people are respected and cared for by the family. The elders are considered valuable because of their age, knowledge and wisdom.

Africans describe distance as, 'Not far', which could be ten miles to an American. Africans are very fit from all the work and exercise of doing basic chores. The big expression in Africa is 'No problem'. Maybe it's no problem for them, but I wouldn't want to walk ten miles in the smelting temperature for anything.

We were anxious to visit Juffureh. It became a major tourist destination during the 1970's after Alex Haley's 'Roots' television mega-drama. Before arriving at Juffureh, we visited the small village of Alberta that is on the shoulder of the Banjul river. Along the coastline still stands a slave castle in disrepair. I asked if the castle was an undertaking of UNESCO? Our guide said, "Not yet". To my surprise a cannon from the 1700's stands on the shore pointed towards the river, the cannons were used to fight off the enemies of the past.

The people of the village gathered around us for a big welcome and accompanied us along our brief walk to a baobab tree where the guide gave us a short lecture on how Africans were captured. Just a short distance across the river is the island of St. James. During the years of the slave trade, captives were incarcerated on the island with a ball and chain to wait to be shipped to the Americas. It was said, that captives were challenged to swim across the river. When they arrived, they must touch the tree stump on the shore in order to gain freedom. Well, no one ever completed the swim. Several children asked for a Bic pen, one boy asked for a watch, so he could arrive at school on time. I gave him a calculator because I didn't have an extra watch.

After departing, we drove a short distance to Kunta Kente village where Alex Haley's ancestors lived. As I stepped from the bus I observed recently built guesthouses with thatched roofs surrounded by bougainvillea on a trellis fence. There are no paved roads, just dirt and dust everywhere. We sat under a thatched roof hut and listen while the interpreter translated for the Queen of the village. She is a distant cousin of Alex Haley. The guide narrated the film 'Roots' from the beginning to where Kunta was captured to the last episode. After the lecture he passed around photographs of famous people who had visited the village. For a small fee, guests received a certificate documenting their visit to the village. I visited a tidy hut with a bed in the middle of the dirt floor. The floor was swept with a homemade straw broom.

On the long return journey to Dakar, our bus landed in soft dirt in front of someone's house. "Who lives here?" someone asked. Along the open savanna from a distance I saw a family of green monkeys with pink behinds. They were playfully jumping from branch to branch in the trees, but they kept their distance.

Many Americans think of Africa as a country, instead of a continent with many countries. Africa has many layers and offers a variety of personalities.

At the end of our tour everyone apologized for their outrageous and demanding behavior at the border the day before. They told me they shared the most wonderful time. It was a long journey but worth every minute of the adventure and laughs.

Ghana

Left: Kings Palace in Kumasi, Ghana

Woman with baby on back

On a catwalk 150 feet up

University of Ghana, Accra

Right: Kwame Nkrumah statue first president of Ghana

Chapter 4
Accra, Ghana

After a nine-hour flight on Ghana Airways, I arrived in Accra, the capital city of Ghana. From the moment I stepped out of the plane, I felt the warmth of the people. They greeted me with a hearty "AWAABA" (welcome), and a warm, friendly, smile. A gap between the front teeth is a sign of great beauty. There are bustling boulevards of commerce and colorful rhythms of life, from the vastness of its land to its marketplaces to the beaches. The people of Ghana love to barter in the craft markets. Ghana, once a British Colony has enjoyed its independence since March 6, 1957. The founding father, President Kwame Nkrumah, made great strides after freeing his country. English is the official language along with twenty-five other indigenous languages and numerous dialects. The currency is the Cedi; the value fluctuates daily. At this writing, 3,000 Cedis equals $1.00 US.

The Gold Coast

Ghana, formally known as the Gold Coast, has many rich natural resources such as gold, diamonds, maganese and bauxite. As quietly as it's kept, Ghana has a gold reserve that's greater than South Africa. The gold mining is being revitalized to make a consistent source of income for the country. Some of the locals in the Ashanti-region gold producing towns do their own prospecting. Sometimes they get lucky. Ghana is the size of Oregon and has 14 million inhabitants with a rich cultural heritage, history and tradition. Ghana is also the home of the Kente Cloth. The city of Kumasi is the seat of the famous Ashanti Kingdom. The Ashanti Warriors fought off the British throughout the early 19th century. Finally, the British were subdued in 1901.

There are several four star hotels that offer all the amenities of home. Some are located on the beach and others in town. I prefer town because it's more convenient for shopping for all those wonderful gifts to impress my friends when I return home.

I toured the University of Ghana, National Museum, Art Center, and W.E.B. DeBois Center for Pan African Culture, Kwame Nkrumah Memorial Park and the craft markets, where woodcarvings are plentiful. I also learned about Ghanaian traditions with a visit to a coffin maker and a herbal doctor, formally known as the 'Witch Doctor' or 'Voodoo Man'. He is the man to visit for natural cures. The coffin makers are very creative with their woodcarving. They will carve a coffin reflecting your profession. For instance, a rich man might have requested an airplane or a pianist, a piano, or a farmer, a pepper. Imagine being put away in such an elaborate fashion!

The women in the craft markets are very aggressive with handshakes and warm smiles. They wear woven Kente cloth wrapped around their hips and over their shoulders. Kente cloth is the traditional cloth of kings. It's woven in five-inch colorful strips sewn together. Each village has its own color combination.

In the Central Region, there is a natural green forest with seven, suspended, narrow swaying catwalks. The walks rest between a row of tall, narrow trees, 150 feet above a collection of untamed animals that sashay freely below. This walk unnerved my last nerve as it began to sway from left to right. I felt as if I was on a tightrope. But once I began, there was no turning back. I inhaled the aromatic fragrance of the unspoiled eucalyptus trees from below.

The Slave Castles

In addition to the country's marketplaces and lush beaches, Ghana has the largest number of slave castles along the Atlantic coast. The city of Elmina, is located in the central region of Ghana along the Atlantic Ocean. The Dutch and Portuguese originally built the Elmina Castle as a trading station and fort to prevent invasions along the coast. It was converted into holding dungeons where slaves were tortured, detained and put to death. There is a small building in the center court, which was originally constructed as a church to convert the Africans to Catholicism. The church was later converted into an auction house for slave trade. White traders peeked through small holes in the wall to be sure of getting what they had paid for.

I walked the tormented historic path of slaves and suddenly fell to my knees with empathy. As I continued the tour of the castle, my heart filled with mountains of emotions and I began to weep. I couldn't fight back the tears streaming down my face. The stench of death permeated the rooms still, after all those years. Men and women were kept in separate cells and the defiant men were separated into an isolated cell with a skull and crossbones over the door. There was no ventilation. It was called "The death from hell cell."

I also toured the upstairs slave traders quarters where young slave girls were lured and seduced. The travesty of 150 years ago has passed, but we have an obligation as people to educate future generations about what happened.

Suddenly, from an open French shutter, a young man climbing a palm tree to get a coconut diverted my attention. He was wearing only shorts. From another window, I heard the rumbling sound of a noisy crowd outside in an open field, watching a collection of young men playing soccer while they cheered them on. Anchored in the harbor were idle, colorfully designed fishermen boats bobbing to the rhythm of the swells. This is a land of contrasts.

Kumasi is located 168 miles north of Accra. It's a beautiful city with lots of tradition. King of the Ashanti, the late Asantehene Osumfuo Opoku Ware II, lives in both the traditional and modern worlds. He is a lawyer by profession. He celebrated his twentieth anniversary on the Golden Stool in 1990. The Gold Stool is the ultimate symbol of Ashanti nationhood. It is the throne of the Ashanti King and the symbol of his office. Many people believe it contains the Sunsum or Souls of all the Ashanti.

I only had time to visit two nearby villages, Ntonso and Bonwire. Ntonso is known for its Adinkra cloth, Ghana's other great fabric. Adinke is colored with brewed bark and root dyes. The traditional Adinke symbols, hand stamped onto the fabric represent proverbs that are also intended to console.

Crafts and Markets

Bonwire has several craft markets of woodcarvings. There I discovered boys sitting and weaving extended lengths of Kente strips under a shaded roof. Kente cloth was originally reserved for the King. The prices are very affordable. There are many markets located on both sides of what appears to be the longest and straightest road I've ever seen.

Kumasi city has the world's largest open-air market where one could get lost for years. Women are seen transporting richly woven cloth atop their heads or trays of fruit and other fresh produce. In the Ga language, the Osu Night market is a Supermakola which means "I'm going to pick a piece of your fire (a hot coal from the open grill) to make some fire of my own."

I toured the Kings Palace in the heart of Kumasi. It was formally a British embassy. The personalized guided tour reviewed all the late kings' memorabilia. On the lawn were large peacocks that spread their feathers whenever they felt like it. They looked as if they should belong to a king.

When I returned to Accra, I visited the Jazz Courtyard at the Balm Pub. There is also an indoor disco, but it was just too noisy for me. I wanted to sit and relax after a busy day. I struck up a conversation with a group of young locals under the starlit African sky. They talked about their culture and dreams. The warmth of the people makes it easy to say hello. One young man stood up after a few Mamba beers and said, "Stand tall; always stand tall."

Ghanaian food is inexpensive and similar to American Southern cuisine. Some dishes look terrible, but WOW!...they taste unbelievably good.

The people are so friendly, gentle and inviting, I want to return again and again. It's an extraordinary experience that has to be shared with friends and family.

Egypt

View from suite at the Mena House Hotel, Cairo

Camel and pyramids in Cairo, Egypt

Egyptian Tourist Police in Cairo at the Pyramids

Philae Temple in Aswan

Abu Simble, Egypt
Temple of Ramses II

Chapter 5
Egypt: The Land of Pharaohs, Kings and Queens

I was inspired and stimulated about returning to Egypt, one of my favorite destinations. While flying on EgyptAir non-stop to Cairo, I slept most of the ten hours. But the real highlight was an invitation into the cockpit with the Captain Ehab A. Elaziz and his first officer, Neveen Darwish, to witness the descent of the plane. The captain has been with Egyptair for forty years and Neveen is a mother of two and has been working with the airline for six. She informed me that Egyptair has eight females as first pilots and one as a captain. I felt like a child bursting with excitement. I sat quietly, mesmerized by the aerial perspective of the Mediterranean Sea and the Giza Pyramids.

Mohamed Ali Amin and Yousreya Ismail from the Egyptian Tourist Authority met us. The MISR tour service escorted us to the Mena House Oberoi Hotel, which is located at the foot of the Giza Pyramids. The Mena House was originally a royal lodge. Khedive Ismail used it as a rest house for himself and his guests when they wanted to hunt in the desert or visit the pyramids across the street. It's my favorite hotel in Cairo. There are lush fauna gardens with an Olympic sized pool, golf and tennis course, a casino, disco, several restaurants, cabaret and a bundle of amenities. Rajiv Kaul (Vice President and General Manager) and Tarek Lotfy (Assistant Director of Sales) cordially greeted us with a welcome drink. The hotel has a vast history of visiting royalty and celebrities. The wandering Islamic design hallways led us to various suites. My suite was accompanied with two terraces looking directly at the pyramids as they stared back. I didn't know which terrace to stand on, so I alternated. Every room in my suite was filled with chocolates, fresh flowers from the garden and fruit. Each night, one fresh rose was placed on my pillow.

The first afternoon, I took a little settling-in time. I wore a blue hotel robe and met several others wearing the same as they were walking toward the pool for a cool dip. Instead of swimming the length, I swam around the pool, recalling my last visit and all the pleasure it brought me. The pool attendants were very attentive and stood erect under the swaying palm trees with the sun peering through. They offered cocktails and carefully placed yellow towels over the chaises.

The first dinner was in the Rubbayat Restaurant. The entertainment included a belly dancer and her warriors. After dinner, we retired to Abu Nawas Night Club to listen to a Tom Jones look- and sound- alike perform American songs. I twisted the night away.

Next morning, an early departure to meet with Dr. Zahi Hawass, director of the Pyramids in Giza. He elaborated on preserving the pyramids and the Sphinx. After the lecture, he led a special climb inside the Cheops' Great Pyramid at Giza to the meditation hall. The tunnel was very steep and narrow with a low ceiling. The only way to climb the wooden planks was to bend forward and look down. As I began to climb behind Jessica O'Keefe from Egyptair, she turned and remarked, "I don't think I want to do this." After her observation, I directed my head forward and suddenly I became claustrophobic. I had second thoughts and descended immediately.

Another highlight was walking around the base of the Sphinx, which is not offered to most visitors. The Sphinx is so massive; it's set against the background of the pyramids as if it's protecting the sacred grounds. I was really impressed. Later that evening, we returned for the sound and light show to see and hear the story of ancient Egypt.

Next morning, we departed for a city tour through the City of the Dead, where a colony of people, live amongst the tombs. Then it was onward to the Museum of Antiquities, which has the most extensive and extraordinary collection of King Tut's treasures. After our extensive visit, we ventured into another one of my favorite places, the Khan El-Khalili markets, to shop and haggle for the best prices on gold, silver, pearlized boxes, scarves, leather wallets, etc. After lunch at the Naguib Mahfouz Café, we visited a perfume factory where glass blowers create beautiful bottles for the perfume. We were given a demonstration on the essential oils and how they were used in ancient times. The salesman stated, "There are three places on the body that perfume is placed." He demonstrated, "Behind each ear on the center of the forehead."

One cannot visit Egypt without a visit to a papyrus shop. We were walked through the process of making of papyrus paper. The gentleman sliced the outer layer away, then sliced the interior of the papyrus plant into thin slivers. He soaked the plant in water for a few days to soften and make it applicable for the cross layering process. On the gallery walls were paintings on papyrus depicting ancient Egypt and its many treasures.

We also visited a carpet school where small children worked diligently constructing magnificent silk and wool carpets. They were animated and their little fingers were very flexible and moved at a rapid pace. I call this process "working your fingers to the bone." After a tour of the factory, we entered the showroom where carpets are offered for sale.

After a long day of touring, when we were returning to the hotel, a soccer game had just ended. The Egyptians are very emotional about their national game. We were rushed by a mob of young men who had attended the game. As we tried passing through the crowd, they rocked our vehicle and I panicked and thought "Oh my God!" They were more enthusiastic than I could ever imagine. Finally, when we passed through the enormous crowd; I let out a sigh of relief.

The Mena House Hotel held a cocktail reception in the garden next to the pool, with a very romantic violin player sharing his music. He was very passionate about his playing.

To visit Cairo without a two-hour dinner cruise is unforgivable. Our boat circled the Nile while Asmaham, a very beautiful and talented belly dancer, entertained us. She was carried in a caravan onto the dance floor by four strong folkloric dancers. After they lowered the caravan and dramatically opened the curtains, she emerged with a bump and a grind. She seduced the entire audience with that certain mysterious look in her eyes. When she looked at me, I felt that I was the only person in the room. She even seduced me to the dance floor and I danced like never before.

The final night at the Mena House was exceptional. A cocktail reception was held on the terrace overlooking the great pyramids. Dinner was prepared and served in the lush garden by the Mohul Indian Restaurant.

As I was departing the hotel for an early short flight to Luxor, I extended my arms and informed the manager that I felt very much at home while staying at the Mena House.

Looking from my window of the plane, I saw fertile land surrounding the Nile and desert beyond. The Nile actually flows north. Egyptians refer to it as flowing to lower Egypt. Upper Egypt is south, where the Egyptian civilization began. We arrived in Luxor and were escorted to the Oberoi Philae Nile Cruiser for a five-day cruise up the Nile. After checking into my suite, which had a terrace overlooking the Nile, a buffet lunch was in order, including freshly cut slivers of watermelon. I swear the best melon is served on the Nile.

After lunch, everyone lounged on the upper deck for a leisurely afternoon. The deck was partially shaded by large white umbrellas. In the middle of the deck was a pool surrounded by lots of chaise lounges covered with yellow and white towels. Once the temperature cooled down, we toured the Karnak and Luxor temples with our Egyptologist, who translated the hieroglyphics on the walls of the temples. Later, we returned to the ship for an afternoon tea and cocktails.

Dinner was à la carte including sautéed steak or chicken with fresh vegetables and a rush of desserts, including flan. After dinner, the evening continued in the ballroom with more cocktails. There were all kinds of colorful characters on board for whom I designed nicknames:

▼ 'Diamond Lil' – wore a diamond as large as a grapefruit. Her entourage included her three children, a nanny, her decorator and her dermatologist's wife.

▼ 'The Ice Queen' – from Germany, who never smiled

▼ 'The Britts' – a witty, dry humored couple from England

▼ 'Mr. Hollywood' – dressed like George Hamilton with sunglasses or Bea Arthur with a turban.

▼ 'The boys' – a gay couple from Toronto

▼ 'Captain Geo' – Captain George

▼ 'Dough Boy' – our Egyptologist was plump

▼ 'Oh, Mama' – Omayma from the Egyptian Tourist Authority

▼ 'Anal retentive' – she loosened up by the end of the cruise

▼ 'Drag Queen' – butch boy, wore a dress at final night jallabaya party. He shocked everyone

▼ 'My first wife' – a young lady I met on the airplane and adopted her as my first wife

I passed the time lazily on a chaise while ordering a Karkaday (cock-a-day), which is hibiscus, juice. I designed a 'Cleopatra on the Nile' drink which consists of several ice cubes in a tall glass, a splash of Vodka, lots of Karkaday, and a tiny splash of orange juice, topped off with another splash of vodka, and please don't stir. Under the hot sun, one can consume an ample amount of them without realizing how relaxing they are.

The temperature is always hot in Egypt. That's why I can't comprehend Muslim women wearing all black clothing wrapped from head to toe. I took frequent dips in the pool to cool off from the sunrays. The coastline along the Nile was absolutely unbelievable because of varied personalities. I observed men farming, camel and horses drinking from the Nile, small towns and villages and lots of temples and large cities along the way.

The Valley of the Kings and Queens is located on the West Bank. During my last visit, I boarded a ferry for a short ride across the river. However, this time we were driven over a very long bridge to the tombs of Nefetari, Tut, and Ramses I, III and III. The most impressive feature is the brilliance of the color of the mural and relief on the walls. Some appear as if they were just completed, but historians assured us that they are remains of five thousand years. A short drive away stands the grand tomb of Queen Hatshepsut. It's carved into the mountainside.

I gathered an eclectic group of new friends and asked the captain of the dining room to extend the tables to look like the "Last Supper." He responded, "we have never had this request before and I don't think we can handle it." I stated, "I'll sacrifice my dinner if necessary." All was done in great style and everyone shared great travel adventures.

One morning 'Diamond Lil' didn't come to breakfast. I asked her 14-year-old son, "What's your mom doing? Polishing her diamonds?" I also told him if he didn't behave, I would ship him to work in one of the carpet factories. "Did my mom tell you that?" he queried. Several guys hung out with me and boarded another ship for a game or two of pool. Of course, we let the youngster win.

Our voyage allowed us to explore Edfu, Esna and Kom Ombo. There were temples and more temples to visit and to learn more about Egyptian history. On one occasion, we rode in a horse drawn carriage to the temple of Esna. There were markets everywhere. I negotiated for a walking stick and got the seller down from 100 pounds to 20. Then several people took advantage of the price.

During my last cruise, while waiting at the locks in Esna, a band of men in rowboats approached our ship displaying beautiful jallabayas for sale. I called this the floating boutique. If you liked the item, they would place it in a bag and toss it to the upper level of the boat. You were obliged to place your money in the bag and toss it back. I waited with anticipation, but it didn't happen on this trip.

As we were approaching Aswan, my eyes overflowed with the joy of returning to this magnificent city with lush hotels such as the Oberoi Philae and the Old Cataract. "Death on the Nile" was filmed at the Cataract. Our tour included the unfinished Obelisk, the Philae Temple, which took three years to move to a higher island to prevent flooding, the Great Damn, and souks with shops.

I took a twenty-five minute plane ride to Abu Simble to view Ramses II and Nefetari's Temples. The flight attendants informed me that I would have an aerial view of the temples if I sat on the left side of the plane. I was most impressed by the mammoth size of the structures. The temples had been moved to a higher plain in order to open the damn and prevent the overflow of the Nazar River onto the temples. The Egyptians took four years to cut, move and reassemble the temples. The interior has impressive remnants of sepia skin tones from five thousand years ago. In Nefetari's temple, there are columns with heads of women with a flip hair style and one wall has a pornographic relief of a man with an erection.

After a long, hot day, we took a peaceful ride in a felucca up and across the Nile with only the sound of the sails fluttering against the wind. The captain and his mates encouraged everyone to join in the local songs and dance on the deck.

Later we explored the souks, where every vendor wants you to look in his shop. There are displays of spices, sheesha pipes, herbal teas, tea shirts, jallabayas, tote bags, etc. Several tourists took a moment to smoke sheesha. Sheesha is a water pipe with assorted fruit flavored tobacco and molasses. I preferred playing dominos with the locals, having hibiscus tea and laughing.

The Oberoi Philae hotel on Elephantine Island is a refreshing treat away from the hustle of the center of town. Yet it's a short ferry ride across the Nile. On one of my many crossings, I was invited to the helm to steer the boat to the opposite shore. I brought it in without incident. The hotel is a little isolated, but has all the amenities to entertain. There is a health spa/gym, Olympic sized pool, dining rooms, shops, bank etc. We celebrated our last night in Aswan with a barbecue dinner over the pool. The sky was filled with the moon and bright Egyptian stars. My suite had a terrace overlooking the Nile and Agha Kahn Mausoleum. Unfortunately, I was so busy trying to absorb everything that I didn't have time to step out and smell the hibiscus.

After a short plane ride to Cairo, we boarded another plane direct to Sharm El Sheikh on the Red Sea. As our car was approaching the Conrad Hotel, its exterior didn't impress me until I entered the property. The hotel had spacious accommodations and sprawling grounds located directly on the sea. We received a welcome fruit juice drink. Muslims never include alcohol in their drinks.

I was expecting to see a Red Sea, but what I saw was the most beautiful turquoise and aqua waters. Someone informed me that it's called the Red Sea because of the red coral and the red reflection of the mountains towards sunset.

Sharm El Sheikh is rapidly developing into a major resort. Hotels are plentiful along the coastline, while across the road is nothing but desert. It's a very surreal environment. Each hotel is self-contained with all the amenities of any five star hotel including shops, a bank and a health club/spa. I participated in an exercise class of jumping up and down and stretching from side to side in the pool with a bunch of young Italian ladies. The evening activities included a cabaret act in the lounge and a disco to dance the night away.

The Red Sea is also known for diving, snorkeling and sea life. Diving clubs offer lessons and certification and one can qualify after three consecutive days. In order to dive, you have to present a certification license, and then they make you sign your life away.

The harbor was congested with boats filled with divers. While crossing the sea, we witnessed dolphins joyfully playing and showing off. Once out at sea, we dropped anchor and another boat attached itself to our boat. Each boat was chartered by a different cordial group of people. I stepped from one boat to the other. Later I ventured off the boat to test the waters for a little snorkeling, since I'm not a strong swimmer. Halfway in to shore which seemed like a million miles away, someone reminded me of the 1,000 foot depth I was floating on. I suddenly panicked and threw my mask into the water. It sank to the bottom as I returned to the boat. For the rest of the day, I just chilled on the upper deck. Lunch was prepared on board and consisted of fresh fried fish, salad, watermelon and oranges with soft drinks. I was so dehydrated that I devoured ten small cokes.

When I returned to shore, I had to pay $70.00 U.S. for the mask. But, hey, it was either the mask or me. When the deep-sea divers returned to the boat to share their underwater stories and adventures, I just listened.

The diving clubs offer two dives per day, one in the morning, the other in the afternoon. They also conduct evening dives for advanced divers.

It was billed as 'Dinner in the Desert'. The guide explained the history of the Bedouins as nomads of the land. We arrived in the desert and were ushered to a designated spot on the laid array of beautiful woven carpets and candlelight. There was also a tent a short distance away. The minute we sat, the merchants began offering items for sale, such as herbal teas. Finally someone asked, "How much do we have to buy in order to get dinner?" I held my dish in front of a candle, but didn't recognize what I was eating. I believe it was chicken, rice and other assorted dishes. After dinner, the guide asked us to lay back and look up at the stars. The sky was clear and the stars were bright. I closed my eyes and began to relax. Then suddenly, someone yelled, "A fox." The guide suggested we scurry to the bus as quickly and as quietly as possible. I was cynical and stated, "I bet they pushed a button for the fox to run out and scare the customers. That way they can bring the next set of tourists and turn the tables three times during the evening to make a profit like the restaurants in New York City."

I spent my last day relaxing on a chaise under the beaming sun on the beach in front of the hotel while sipping ice tea and munching on slices of watermelon. This is my idea of living.

Upon departing the hotel, I panicked, because I had forgotten the combination to my safe. It contained my money, passport and credit cards. Fortunately, the manager was able to open it. I was so relieved. I rushed out of the hotel and forgot to pack my film, shirt and bathing suit. Sara Zimmerman, a journalist from New York (I called her my first wife, because it was easier to remember than Sara) was staying an extra two days. So when I returned home, I called her and asked to check with housekeeping. Sure enough, she returned home with the items.

Now as I reflect on the thirteen days I spent in Egypt, I had flown on eight planes and spent four nights on the Nile cruise. I was exhausted, but it was the most exhilarating, humorous and exciting adventure I've shared anywhere around the world.

Spiritual Healing and Nubian Heritage in Egypt

I hosted a group of African/Americans from across the United States to Egypt on EgyptAir for a spiritual healing and Nubian heritage tour. I was awakened each morning at 4:30 a.m. by an amplified Azan (call to prayer) for all Egyptian Muslims. There are five daily calls: sunrise, midday, afternoon, sunset and during the evening. Each morning, the call rang into my suite at the Mena House Hotel in Cairo through the terrace door. As I opened the door, I viewed the magic of the Great Pyramids just across the road, staring back at me.

Each day at the crack of dawn, just before the sun began to rise, we were transferred by bus to a historical site before it became congested with tourists. Our first stop was in the Giza where the Sphinx stands guard at the Pyramids. We gathered in front of the Sphinx, formed a circle and held hands, then took a long deep inhalation to start the day. I led the group with three long chants of ohms. After the ohms, we took a silent moment to reflect on our being one. The morning dew filled the air and there was only the sound of the morning wind and occasionally a bird or a camel trotting by. From within, I felt a sense of peace and tranquility and all my problems seemed to have vanished. I was ready to accept any new challenges. I think everyone in the group felt the same way. This was not a religious experience, but a spiritual healing. We were getting in touch with our most inner self. The experience placed us solidly on the ground so that we could focus and continue to make our lives fuller. Our Egyptologist brother, Emil Shaker, and sister, Amal Shallan from Quest Travel were very passionate regarding our Black Heritage. They spent countless hours sharing their enthusiasm and knowledge of the Nubian history of Egypt.

As we marched from one sight to another, Emil would yell out, "Be one," which reflected the mood of the day. To me, it meant being in touch with my feelings and released the pressures of my daily life. Half of the group climbed inside the great pyramid to the meditation chamber. I passed on that experience, because I am claustrophobic, and climbing into that steep passageway would have been disastrous for me. I tried it once before, but couldn't get beyond ten steps inside. It seemed that the world was closing in on me and I couldn't get out. But I was later informed that the spiritual feeling of reaching the chamber at the top and spending time meditating in silence and solitude was the experience of a lifetime.

All of the temples we visited are located along the Nile River where the land is fertile. Beyond the Nile River is a vast desert with sand and camels. Several people boarded camels for a trot along the desert. Emil informed me that the temples were built like human bodies: the court where the Pharaoh's subjects congregated was like the legs of a human and the body was the center court, and finally, the head was for the high priest. The temples were also acoustics chambers without any modern amplification. As we joined together for our daily chants, I heard the ringing of our ohms throughout the temples. The temples were built with grand style; some with papyrus leaf capitals on fluted columns and some plain columns with lotus capitals. These columns dwarf man. Walking within the walls of these temples placed me in another time and place. It was easy to surrender my soul and mediate each morning at dawn.

Aswan is located in Upper Egypt. It is also south where the Egyptian civilization began. Cairo and Alexandria are in the north, which is called Lower Egypt. There are only two rivers in the world that flow north—St. John's (in Florida) and the Nile. After departing Cairo, we flew down to Aswan and boarded the Nile Goddess Cruiser in Aswan for a four-night journey down the Nile to Luxor. This was the opposite direction of my previous journeys. The temperature in Aswan and Luxor is hotter because of its southern location. The Nubian population dominates the south. The locals often called me Nubian because of my dark skin. Aswan has the largest Nubian museum, which contains many elements of the Nubian civilization. I was quite impressed with the entire collection and its history. It's a must see on any trip to Aswan. The museum brought a better understanding of their culture and history. The most amazing thing was walking through the paths of the museum where time seem to revert itself into the past. The building is very large and modern, but the exhibit is massive and culturally inspiring. There are village scenes, artifacts, alabaster statues, baskets, archeological findings, etc.

The tour was designed to crescendo from the beautiful Philae Temple in Aswan, which had been moved to a higher plain to prevent flooding from the dam, to the Karnak temple in Luxor, which is the largest temple in Egypt. It was built in three parts. Emil took us into the temple of the Black god where he requested the guard to close the front door so we could have solitude and reflect on the resonate sound and vibes of the temple. We closed our eyes and repeated our ohms. I felt warmth around my face, with someone pressing down on my shoulders. At one point I felt something very close to me that gently kissed me on my lips.

Late one afternoon, we boarded a felucca (sailboat) and sailed up and down the Nile humming a Nubian song. While everyone clapped and joined in for a little shake your booty time, I stretched out on the bow of the boat, focusing on my surroundings. I snapped photographs while the sails fluttered in the wind as the boat splashed gently against the soft swells. Small boys rushed our felucca in their colorful homemade wooden paddleboats while singing western songs and requesting baksheesh (tips). I have visited Egypt six times, and each time, I see it with a different eye. Egypt is a country that I never tire of because it has so many layers to uncover.

Morroco

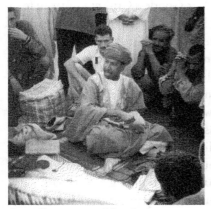

Storyteller in square, Marrakech

Guerabs in square, Marrakech

Women weaving carpets in Marrakech

Snake charmer in
square, Marrakech

Minnerette in Marrakech

Chapter 6
The Magic and Mystery of Morocco

Just the mere thought of two words, "Magic & Mystery" and the phrase, "Take me to the Kasbah" intrigued me to visit Morocco. Benjaafar Marrakshi, the USA director for the Moroccan National Tourist Office, designed my ten-day tour.

I boarded a Royal Air Maroc Boeing 747-400 to Casablanca. The jumbo jet had a seating capacity of 470. I was impressed with the courteous, efficient and pleasant staff. Royal Air Maroc served the best airplane food I've ever tasted. I felt as if I was on a magic carpet.

Morocco is on the northwest coast of Africa. As we were nearing our destination, I lifted the shade and peeked from the window and just beyond the horizon waited a beautiful sky of gray, blue and orange colors at dawn. Morocco's time difference is four hours ahead of New York.

After a six and half-hour flight, we landed at Mohammed V Airport in Casablanca (what a romantic nostalgic sound), for a connecting flight to Agadir. The high season to travel to Morocco is from March through August.

Landing in Agadir gave me the first taste of the country. Agadir is a coastal town on the Atlantic that was totally destroyed by an earthquake and then rebuilt in 1961. The temperature was hot—perfect for me.

Islam is the religion of the majority. As we exited the airport terminal, I was surprised by an enormous, rushing crowd of men dressed in white.

They were returning from Mecca where they had made the Hajj (the trip that every Muslim strives to make, at least once in a lifetime). A crush of people was waiting on the street while being restrained by the police. They were anxious to meet returning friends and relatives.

I met Abdelghani Abdu El Kochta, our driver shortly after I arrived. He spoke English, French and Arabic. We met shortly after my arrival in Agadir. He had a great sense of humor, an infectious smile, and he loved to laugh. His knowledge and wisdom helped me understand the vast culture of the country and made my tour exciting and educational. He was part of the Magic of Morocco.

After I checked in at the Hotel Anezi (means a small village outside of Agadir), I dashed to lunch at the outdoor cafe in the courtyard next to the pool. I dined on fresh fish, salad, fruits and crème caramel for desert then chased it down with a large cool bottle of Flag Beer. Although alcohol is available in this Muslim country, their national drink is heavily sweetened mint tea. The Moroccans serve tea everywhere, including shops, where it is offered at the beginning of price negotiations; it's a sign of hospitality.

The long promenade along the beach was inspiring because as I walked, locals greeted me with a warm smile and a sincere welcome. The hotel was a stone step from the beach. The light honey color sand and aqua water embraced the white swell rushing to the shore.

I observed many young and middle-aged Europeans beaming in the sun, while the body conscious young Agadirians galloped along the beach playing soccer. I just laid on a chaise, shaded by a thatched umbrella, to soak in the essence of the land, sea and sun. I struck up a casual conversation with a mixed race Moroccan waiter and a dark skinned waitress in order to learn about their heritage. They told me that their grandfathers were captured as slaves and transported from Senegal. Others were from neighboring countries on the West Coast or prisoners of war. The French had occupied Morocco from 1912-1956. Slavery was not abolished until 1956.

The city of Safi, was a major coastal slave port. The fortresses still remain after 400 years. Slaves worked on the plantations and built royal palaces and cities for the King.

Many European ladies were topless. But the locals are very conservative and abide by their Islamic faith. Moroccan women dress in white, pastel or black djellabas with a hood draped from the shoulder. They casually cover their feet with yellow babouch. Some wear veils covering their face and a scarf around their head for respect of their religion, while others wear western clothes. I asked why yellow shoes and someone explained that the color coordinates with most colors. Henna is very popular to decorate the hands and it's also used as a decorative touch on the face. If a woman had a painted henna chin and forehead, it means she is married.

Morocco has an eclectic population of thirty million, Arabic, Germans, Senegalese, French, Berbers, Gnaonas, etc. Seventy five-percent of the population is under thirty-six years old. The national language is Arabic and French. The King has a royal palace in every major city with miles of thick walls guarding them. Every city has a Medina (old city that was built during the fourteenth century Merimide Dynasty) and a Souk (a shopping mall), with narrow uneven cobblestone streets that are wide enough for a donkey or a motorbike. The streets lead from one shop to another with merchants inviting me in, "Come to my shop with no obligation." There is also a new city, built during the twentieth century.

The Agadir Beach Club Hotel is located directly on the beach. There is a revolving mail and key rack in the lobby that fascinated me. The suites are built around a circle – all with ocean views. There are many sports activities to participate in at each hotel. Doormen, wear typical Moroccan wear, such as a burgundy Fez hat with a tassel (the Fez hat was originally brought from Tunisia to Turkey and then to Morocco), white pantaloons, decorative vest and shirt and those yellow sheepskin pointed slippers (babouch).

I had the feeling I was in Paris because there were bistros and grand boulevards everywhere. The bistros gave me an opportunity to get acquainted with the locals. One night, I was sharing dinner with a friend, and at the next table, sat four people, two locals and two Germans. The environment stimulated a conversation. Suddenly I found myself in the midst of outrageous laughter. The locals have a great sense of humor. That's why I say: "First, pack a sense of humor before traveling. The night continued and I continued to hold court with surrounding tables.

Next morning, we departed for the long, long winding, two-lane road around and through the Atlas Mountains (Zerthoume). The Berbers live in the high Atlas Mountains. Their isolation is extreme; they have not been ruled by outside powers in over 1,000 years and still lead an existence on the fringes of the Moroccan State, receiving no benefits and paying no taxes. The family is the cornerstone of the Berber life.

From a distance, I saw a collection of snow-capped mountains. The countryside was filled with fertile rolling hills and plains. At one point I asked Abdu to stop the car so I could photograph the scenery. He parked too close to the edge for my taste. I refused to step out for fear that I would land on the rooftops of the village below. The road was congested with Mercedes taxis, mules, mopeds, donkeys and horses. There were also donkeys and cows being transported in the back of open-air trucks.

The drive through the countryside was an exhilarating experience. During the long ride, we stopped along at a roadside stand to sample, fresh killed lamb. The butcher displayed a lamb on a hook, he asked me to select the cut; then chopped it off and threw it on the grill. "Oh! That'll kill the flies," I remarked. I actually enjoyed eating the lamb chops and fresh baked bread with my hands. I complemented my meal with a glass of very, sweet, mint tea.

After an eight-hour drive, we arrived in Marrakech. The buildings are painted coral, with patina window trimming. Our hotel, The Palmeraie Golf Palace, is a lush, palatial self-contained estate with 350 suites. Some of the amenities include an eighteen-hole golf course and horseback riding. They even have a five story water slide that I climbed and asked myself, "What am I doing up here?" It was too late. I simply sat down, closed my eyes, and then went for the plunge. I felt as if I was on a bobsled spiraling in five directions at once. Suddenly I abruptly landed in the pool.

There were also five restaurants, a disco, piano bar, five swimming pools (one heated) and chocolates on my pillow. The Moroccan Narjis Restaurant had an animated floorshow of musicians and two belly dancers. One danced with lighted candles on a tray over her head. The other dancer shook up the room with her isolated movements and an infectious smile. The dancers mesmerized me, so the food became secondary.

Marrakech is really two cities; old city behind the wall and the new city that is continuing to develop with first class accommodations. The Souk is located behind the old walls and it dates back to the ninth century. The Main Square, or Place Djemaa el Fna (congregation of the departed) resembled a movie set with lots of action. People coming and going

104

twenty four hours a day. It appeared that the entire city congregated in the square. Tourist buses unloaded their guests in front of Brasserie du Glacier. It was endless traffic. Uniformed policemen patrolled at busy intersections.

During the day, the temperature was unbearably hot and the square wasn't as populated, but starting early evening when the temperature dropped, the entire city descended upon the square. The streets are filled with motorbikes, Mercedes and petit cabs. The city provides parking lots for motorbikes, of course for a small fee. On several occasions I sat in a bistro to observe the crowd. At six o'clock the smoke filled square had an abundance of food vendors who seem to arise from the floor on a magic carpet. They set up shop within minutes and serve their freshly cooked dishes. The air was filtered with aromas of fresh squeezed orange juice, escargot, grilled fish, sausages, herbs and exotic spices.

As I walked from one vendor to the next, I spotted a display of mutton heads on food counters. I watched as the merchant chopped off a small piece and minced it into smaller pieces then served it to customers. I especially liked the smashed eggplant dish, fresh fried fish and chips with a grilled hot pepper. It was accompanied with a loaf of fresh baked bread.

This enormous square was also filled with an eclectic group of animated performers, snake charmers blowing wind instruments, drummers encouraging a snake to stand at attention. Tourists were invited to touch and curl the snake around their neck for a photo opportunity, for which they were asked to pay a small fee. The square was also filled with jugglers and fire eaters, drummers and horn players, street performers, drag-queens, acrobats, fortune tellers, a game of chance with a ring attached to fishing poles. If you're lucky, you can win a large bottle of Coca-Cola. Gerabs (Berbers from the mountains) dressed in traditional colorful costumes to sold cups of fresh water and offered to pose for pictures in exchange for a few coins.

Many shops in the Medina (Sulk) behind the great wall, offer the same merchandise of ceramic dishes, pottery, baskets, silverware, sconces, decorative vases, jewelry, hats, babouch and carpets. Whenever someone asked me for direction, I said, "Follow your shoes." Many friendly vendors hawking their goods invited me into their shop. I commented, "What do you think I am, a tourist? What part of 'No' don't you understand?" Regardless of what I told them, they simply changed the subject and practically pulled me into their shop. I stepped off a narrow cobblestone street into a bakeshop with a brick oven. It was a popular shop for the locals to bring their dough to be baked for 5 cents.

After a six-hour drive to Fez, we checked in at the Hotel Palais Jamai, it's the sister to La Mamounia in Marrakech. Winston Churchill, Ronald Reagan, Whoopi Goldberg and many other stars have stayed at La Mamounia. Abdu told me a story of why Mr. Churchill did not want his initials on his door. Think about it, W.C. The Palais Jamai at one time was the nineteenth century palace of the Vizier to Sultan Moulay Hassan. The hotel had a lovely Andalusian garden that overlooked a large heated swimming pool and two restaurants, French and Moroccan. From the terrace of my suite, I viewed the Medina.

One afternoon, I wandered off to the Medina and stopped at a bistro for mint tea. There were rows of men sitting and facing the street, watching TV and sharing mint tea and conversation. There wasn't a woman in sight. I think it's a man's thing. Moroccans dine after nine p.m. I turned to one young man sitting next to me and asked, "Where do you shop for your tea pots?" He offered a lesson on how to haggle for the right price and directed me to his favorite store. I hopped in a taxi and totally confused the driver. I didn't know whether to go left, right, or about face. The driver stopped short and laughed. I managed to get a few familiar French words from my lips, "Where to buy Tea pot?" At the shop, I negotiated for the democratic price. I think it's more interesting to inquire as to where locals shop because they get the best prices. Sometimes the locations are less colorful, but the price is right.

Just off the square from the Souk, and behind another great wall, was the Palais M'Nebli Restaurant. The door opened onto a wonderful Palace with a large center room. I dined on pastilla (a flaky crust sprinkled with white powdery sugar on the top, filled with raisins and squab, almonds, ginger, cinnamon etc), tagine poulet, couscous and vegetables. After lunch, I was given a guided tour of the Palace. From the rooftop terrace, I viewed the Medina. Then I was guided downstairs to a gallery of carpets. Carpet weaving is so masterful and exquisite. All the colors are made from natural dyes. Kilim rugs are very colorful and tell stories of the Berber village.

When I returned to the hotel, Mr. Youssef Attari, Sales Manager, suggested I try the best Moroccan restaurant in Fez, "La Maison Bleue", for dinner.

As I was escorted from the taxi, the front door appeared to magically open. Several escorts began ringing bells to announce my arrival. While walking down a winding hall, another door opened onto a grand parlor with quadruple height ceilings and a well-dressed gentleman surprised me with a greeting, "Welcome Mr. Jon."

The restaurant was decorated with sofas, candelabras and items of a personal nature, that one would find in a home. Mr. Mehdi El Abbadi, the owner, stated he doesn't have menus because each night there is a different dish that helps to create the ambiance of visiting someone's home. Actually this was his home. All the tablecloths were sprinkled with rose petals. My table was also decorated with sparkling sequins spelling my name. I dined on assorted appetizers, tagine lamb and couscous with vegetables. A luscious, very thin layered, flaky crust, filled with creme pudding dessert was devoured very quickly.

A trio of Gnaonas (from the southern region of Morocco) played music related to their combination of old Gnaona religion and Islam (God and the Prophets). One of the musicians twirled a tassel attached to his cowrie shell beaded cap, stamped, and kicked his feet and snapped castanets all at the same time. He was busy.

Next morning, I took a scenic route from Fez to Meknes. Fez, Meknes, Rabat and Marrakech are the four Imperial cities of Morocco. While driving up and around the mountainside, the road was crowded with horses, goats and cows. From the window of the car, I saw planes and colorful rolling hills, with aisles of olive trees and wild flowers, poppies and hibiscus in full bloom creating an intricate tapestry pattern. Men rode donkeys sidesaddle along the road, with their provisions in woven baskets. From a distance, the villages appeared peaceful and tranquil. While some men lazed in the shade along the road.

We toured the city of Meknes where King Moulay Ismail, built palaces with three massive thick walls during the 17th century. The walls stood 26 to 32 feet high and surround the city. King Ismail, was the great grandfather of the present King. The King also owned 80,000 Berber, Black and Arabic Slaves, who built his palaces and tiled the sidewalks in every major city.

As we drove through the city of Volubilis, I saw Roman Ruins, still standing after an earthquake some fourteen centuries ago. There was also a huge open-air outdoor market covered with canvas to protect the perishable products from the sun. There, I found fresh meat, bread, fabric, etc. One of the towns we passed, was so small, it only had one bistro with one table. La Rache, a fisherman's town by the sea, was rather picturesque with houses painted white with blue trim. Each town has its own distinguishing color.

We drove briskly through the town of Rabat, the capital; it was bustling with traffic and commerce. The Bouregreg Rive divides the city. Rabat is the home of the government offices. It's also the home of the King. Every town in Morocco, has a Mohammed V or Houssein II Boulevard, named after its great kings. Rabat is also known as the city of knowledge with its many universities of higher learning.

After a long drive, we arrived in Tangier. Tangier is a major port town with wide beaches and many hotels along the main boulevard. From one vanishing point, I could see where the Atlantic Ocean and the Mediterranean Sea meet. Just eight miles across the sea is Gibraltar, Spain. I would have taken a day trip on the ferry, if I had the time.

I resided at the El Minzah Hotel, one of Morocco's great hotels. The El Minzah Hotel was the center of intrigue during the 1920's. It was most frequented by movie stars and politicians. Mr. Abdelhamid Souab, sales manager, runs this quaint little hotel. He was totally charming and gracious as he escorted me on a tour. He informed me that Lord Butte, an English aristocrat, built the hotel, in 1930. The hotel is located one block from the Souk. The Souk in Tangier is a little different from the others, because it has winding rows of shops on a declining hill to propel you into the shops and help you spend your very last dime. The Souk is a Mecca of shops that inter-twine into a maze, where one could easily lose him or herself.

After departing Tangier, my journey was coming to a close. My last stop was in Casablanca, which is a metropolis of business. Casablanca has a population of five million during the day. As I arrived in town, people were jetting out from hibiscus bushes in every direction into the traffic. I truly got the feeling I was back in New York with the hustle and bustle of the crowded streets.

I stayed at the Royal Mansour Hotel. The hotel is a landmark, built in the 1950's. It has all the modern amenities such as: a health club and a Moroccan and a French restaurant. It's located across the street from the Medina and one block from Rick's Cafe. Remember the movie Casablanca? One of the other main attractions in Casablanca is the new grand Mosque, which is just a short taxi ride from the hotel. It's a massive structure built over the waterfront and has a capacity of forty thousand.

Morocco has all the spices and flavor of life with its diverse culture, tradition, religion, art, craftsmen, humor, beaches, bistros, boulevards, mountains covered in green, and cosmopolitan cities. Morocco is a magical place, because of its history and treasures that are hidden behind great walls. Morocco needs to be discovered and experienced by everyone.

Senegal

Silver and brass in souk

Goree Island

Vendores on street in Dakar

Wooden sculpture

*President's Palace
Dakar, Senegal*

Jon standing in the Door of No Return on Goree Island

The Door of No Return, Goree Island

Men playing talking drums Senegal

Fulani woman watering her crop

The Saloum Delta

Market vendors

Giving books to a school in Senegal

Standing in front of the Presidential Palace in Dakar, Senegal

Jon and a group of 96 who traveled to Dakar, Senegal

Ghana

Elmina Castle, dating from 15th centura, Ghana

Cell for captives in Elmina Castle

Auction house in center of Elmina Castle, Ghana

Elmina Castle

Egypt

Old Cataract Hotel in Aswan

Felluccas on the Nile

Fellucca on Nile in Aswan

Queen Hatshepsuts Temple, Egypt

Brazil

Military Island off the coast of Rio was originally built for the Royal Family

Spices on display

Tower of Castle on Military Island

Mangeria Carnival Costume

Bahia

Street dancers in Pellourinha Square

Hippie Village in Bahia

Hippie Village, Bahia

South Africa

Jonopo village, Umatat, South Africa

Prison on Robben's Island where Nelson Mandela was incarcerated for 27 years

Singiti lodge in Kruger Park

Villagers, Jonopo village, Umtata

Chapter 7
Adventures in South Africa

Blacky Komani, manager of Satour (South African Tourist Board), designed my tour of South Africa. He told me that his parents named him Blacky, so he will never forget who he is. As the 747-400 South African Airlines plane soared through the sky, the clouds and the fertile land below appeared to stand still. Issacs from Leiswai Tours met us at the international airport in Johannesburg and ushered us to The Grace Hotel. The Grace is a five-star hotel with all the amenities of home. And all the little things that make a difference, such as an umbrella and a selection of herbal teas and pale floral arrangements in every spacious suite. Also a lap pool, a sun deck and a restaurant on the fourth floor terrace. The hotel is located in an upwardly mobile, residential neighborhood. From my window, I viewed the peaks and valleys of the mountains. Dinner was served in the English style dining room. I dined on a rack of lamb with a specially prepared appetizer of onion tarts and crab soup, mushroom, ravioli and grilled duck in cherry piecrust. I ordered yogurt and halva mint, pistachio ice cream, for desert.

Because South Africa has such a diverse culture it visualizes tourism as its number one industry in the near future. Stewart Lumba, director of Satour in South Africa, was the host of the first breakfast. I shared some of the best fresh fruits such as: pomegranate, watermelon, apricots and papayas. He stated that South Africa is a whole world in one country. South Africa is working towards better medical services, TV communications, and less crime. He has established a zero tolerance tourism task group for a strong human rights bill. South Africa wants to privatize prison systems, railroads, South African Airways, defense and mining, and perhaps someday participate in one global currency. Tourism will be implemented in schools. He wants political integration of culture and financial government grants for development and to exchange views and ideas and the establishment of partnerships around the world.

The town of Johannesburg is a metropolis of modern skyscrapers that reflect the fast pace of the city. Soccer and cricket are the national sports. There are several large, modern stadiums to exhibit their talents. In the midst of this metropolis, is a Muti shop that sells alternative medicine. The Muti man has remedies for anything that ails you. From the shop's exterior, it appears as a junk store with a variety of items hanging from the ceiling, such as: Ram horns, assorted skins, teeth from various animals, herbal remedies and black dolls etc. The community taxi and municipal buses are the popular mode of inexpensive transportation. In the heart of this metropolis is the Market Theatre. It is Johannesburg's little Hollywood. I met John Kani, an actor, just as I was exiting the theatre. He is the Chairman of the National Art Body. Many productions are produced in the three theaters such as "Five Guys Named Mo," "Bring 'N da Noise, Bring 'N da Funk," "Having Our Say" and sub culture from Soweto. The National Theatre of South Africa produced "Sarafina." They have also included a ballet company and an Opera house. The facility offers laboratory workshops for experimental workshops, very much like Joseph Papp's theatre.

I ordered delicious King Klip (popular local fish), fresh pea pods, carrots and new potatoes for dinner at the Sandton Hilton. The restaurant is in an open atrium with greenery and waterfalls everywhere. For desert, I shared a Trio Diavolo (a devilish trilogy of yogurt ice cream, surrendering to freshly sliced fruits and a rainbow of sauces. South Africans refer to water as being still or sparkling (plain or carbonated).

After dinner I joined several Americans for a nightcap and listened to local music in one of the hotel's public rooms. American music is international, whether it's jazz or pop. Wherever I go around the world, I hear reminders of home.

The Township Of Soweto

Soweto Township is a short drive from Johannesburg. Seventy percent of the gold is mined from dams and the de Beers are the biggest diamond miners in the world. As we toured the countryside, from a distance, I observed several mountains that are being mined. Townships were established for blacks in 1938, Soweto Township is surrounded by mine damns and is located at the outer-rim of the city. The center of the rim was designed for the rich whites. Poor whites live in the second ring and colored (mixed) are in the third. During the month of August (windy season), there is a white cloud of dust that covers the entire southwestern township

Most homes in Soweto are constructed with just two rooms, but as the family expands, they add another room or two. The two rooms are constructed with cinderblocks. They consist of a bedroom and a kitchen with an outdoor toilet. The roof is made of tin and any addition is constructed of tin. South Africans have a very strong extended family relationship. I visited a pre-school where Florence Ntombi Nyathi is the director of Happy Day Pre-school, 3582 Mpane St., Soweto, South Africa 1804. She adopts children who have been abused or abandoned by their family. Unfortunately, some of the children's parents have been killed and the children have nowhere to go except her school. I entered a building and found many children napping on the floor. The children wore tidy school uniforms.

The blacks that live in townships are offered a ninety-nine year lease on their property by the South African government. The lease can be passed down from one generation to another. Eighty-five percent of the population is Christian. Winnie Mandela and Bishop Tutu have large homes in Soweto. Issacs stopped the car in front of Winnie Mandela's mansion. I couldn't see beyond the tall gate that surrounded the house, even when I walked up the hillside for a better view. A short walking distance away from Mrs. Mandela's home is Mr. Mandela's original home where he and Winnie had lived. It's been converted into a national Museum. The tour guide informed me what the colors of the flag represent: red is the blood, green is the land, black is the people, yellow is the wealth and white is for foreigners. There were items depicting Mandela's incarceration on Robben's Island (just off the coast of Cape Town), such as the boots and clothing he wore and items he might have used.

After a quick lunch, we stopped at Hector Peterson's Square. In 1976, Hector was the first black student shot by police in the square during the student protest against Afrikaan (the language). Today standing there is a monument and museum, with devastating photographs by Sam Nzima and Peter Magubane, who witnessed the horror. Viewing the horrific scene in the photographs made it difficult for me to fight back the tears. The photographs reminded me of the horror of Selma, Alabama during the 1960's. There are now eleven official languages in South Africa: English, Xhosa, Zulu Natal, Soto, Tswana, Pedi, Afrikaan, Venda, Shona and Northern Soto. Apartheid was abolished in 1992. In spite of all the oppression, many black and colored South Africans were warm and friendly and shared a sense of humor.

The Adventures of Kruger Park

The flight from Johannesburg to Kruger National Game Reserve in the northeast takes forty-five minutes on a small South African Airline prop plane. We landed in the midst of an open field and were greeted by the baggage handlers and Cole, the driver. Cole has had ten years experience after graduating from the Ranger school and Eco training college. All Rangers travel with a tracker. He sits on a special seat on the left just above the motor. Within minutes, we boarded an eight-seat safari land rover for what I thought would be a short journey to Castleton Game Reserve. Well, as we rode through the wilds, there were giraffes, rhinos, monkeys, spiders, snakes, impalas, deer, lions, zebra, gazelles, buffalo, etc. They were going about their daily business with not the least care of our appearance. On several occasions, I witnessed a lion crossing the road just in front of the rover. These animals are used to vehicles, but not the shape of people so it's best not to stand because they may attack.

Cole informed me that the ride to the lodge was only a few miles up the road. However, after the flight, I was a bit exhausted and began to nap. After a brief nap, as I opened my eyes, I saw a large white lodge rising into the green and blue from afar. When I fully awakened, I realized it was a mere mirage. There was really nothing there but fertile green wilderness and untamed animals. We passed Mala Mala, the largest and most expensive lodge. After another half-hour, we landed at the Singiti lodge. I was greeted with a refreshing welcome drink of tropical fruit juices on an open deck.

Then we were off to Castleton Lodge. There was no television or phone at the lodge to disturb the tranquil state I quickly adjusted to. The accommodations included a pool. The lodge offered two location choices for dinner—the dining room or picnic style at an outdoor table. We chose the outdoors, from where we could observe the wild animals in their natural environment. Dinner was prepared on an open grill—steak, chicken, sausage and lightly barbecued vegetables.

There were eight cabins that can accommodate 16 people. The décor was English and bamboo with African accents. Each suite had a four-poster bed, antelope table legs, pool and Jacuzzi. There were African patterns throughout, with wooden, inlaid, skin pattern, framed mirrors. Castleton will only rent all eight bungalows at one price. This provides a very private facility for a group or friends. Castleton does not accommodate children, for obvious safety reasons.

During the evenings, bugs are attracted to the lights, so we only used a spotlight to observe the movement of the animals.

A herd of buffaloes sashayed across the road and dared us to come closer. I was frightened for only a second. The animals were two feet away. I just couldn't image it being real. I visualized it as a chroma-key blue background with the images projected on the screen, like in television land. But this was very real. There are two scheduled game drives available per day, early morning and evening. Lions hunt at night and by daybreak they are exhausted and rest. It was an UN-BE-LIEV-ABLE experience being in the wilderness.

I felt relaxed after a peaceful night of sounds from crickets, frogs and the stillness of the lagoon. I opened the French doors onto the verandah and sat in a rattan chair padded with English chintz cloth for an early morning breakfast of homemade marmalade on a biscuit, fresh cut fruit and a glass of orange juice. Suspended from the ceiling was a wooden Panama fan slowly cooling the room. From a distance, I saw a spectacular early morning sunrise. Nearby, was a herd of buffalo drinking from the lake. I could clearly see the lush wilderness beyond the horizon. There was a gazebo and swing suspended from a tree at the poolside.

The housekeepers wore white uniforms with a twist wrap of striped African cloth tied into a sarong over their skirt. Some folks may call this the deepest, darkest, part of Africa, but I see it as another state of tranquility, undisturbed, with animals sashaying about their business and me observing their environment. I closed my eyes and thought I had died and gone to heaven. I felt so at peace with myself. I wish I could have stayed at least another night.

The Rolling Hills of Umtata—Mr. Nelson Mandela's Hometown

I asked Blacky if we could visit some locals. He informed me that he had arranged an overnight stay in Jonopo Village. After the most peaceful transition of nothing but the sounds of the wild, we boarded a short flight back to Johannesburg in order to catch a flight to Umtata. The village is located along the side of the throughway. As we entered the village, locals from neighboring villages rushed our vehicle and lifted their voices in song while beating the African drum. They were dressed in costumes that reflected their local area. Upon our arrival, I jumped out of the car and joined in the dance with the children. Thirty families inhabit the village. A precocious little six-year old girl with dancing feet and mobile hips danced with true conviction and dedication. She was totally coordinated from her shoulders to her hips and down to her feet. She wore a colorful cotton skirt that was decorated with beads.

Once the singing and dancing stopped, we were led to their social hut for a formal welcome. Men sat on one side and women on the other. Suddenly, from nowhere, a live chicken was place in front of me as a sign of welcome. Someone informed me that my eyeglasses fogged up from fear and the mere thought that I might have to kill it. After they removed the bird, they passed around light appetizers to whet my appetite, such as corn shucked from the cob (corn is a food staple), barbecued chicken parts etc. For a chaser, a large calabash bowl of home brewed pungent beer was passed around.

The local language is Xhosa. It has a sound of a click and a clack with the tongue before pronouncing various words. The first time I heard that sound was from Miriam Mekeba when she appeared on the Ed Sullivan television show back in the sixties or seventies. The proprietor, a very generous and warm lady, welcomes battered or displaced children. And she doesn't receive any support from the government.

After the ceremonial reception, dinner was served in yet another hut. Unfortunately, I didn't have a big appetite for the assortment of IMIFINO (similar to collard greens), more chicken, and more corn and cassava bread.

The mud huts are circular in shape with a thatched roof. Four men and four women were assigned to a sleeping hut. Each hut had only the bare essentials, such as four beds. To my surprise, the bed was firm as a board. The evening was foggy and it rained; the walkways were muddy and slippery.

The next day, I walked from hut to hut with a large plastic shopping bag requesting all visitors to deposit all the amenities they had taken from the five star hotels. As I handed the owner the bag filled with goodies, she jumped for joy and let out a loud church scream thanking the spirits; it scared me to death.

Umtata is located in the eastern region of South Africa. Men and boys ride horses along the highway. It's an agricultural community with many hills and plains. Umtata is commonly called, the Wild Coast. The village is made up of groups of small dusty rose and tropical colored houses. This is the very town where Mr. Mandela was born and had built a sixteen-room mansion that was designed like the prison where he spent twenty-seven years. It's also a fortress with guards, but we were granted special permission to walk the grounds. We entered a large meeting hall for parties and a smaller meeting room. Parked in the middle of the hall was a four-wheel drive with a license plate #002NRM (Nelson R. Mandela) G. P. Gauteng Provence. That was his retirement home.

A young boy had been killed while crossing the highway in front of Mr. Mandela's estate, so he decided to build an underpath for crossing. Mandela wants to make South Africa safer for everyone. I witnessed several young boys leading herds of sheep along the roadside.

We also met Mandela's brother, Leonard, who toured us through the many cornfields, which suddenly emerged into the gravesite of their mother (Nosekeni Fanny Mandela), father (Chief Mphakanyisma), and sister (Baluve). His father died in the sixties while Mandela was in prison. I was told that when Mandela is in town, he takes early morning walks along the fields.

Zuks repeated an incident about a white man who tried to insult a black man:

"Go to hell," yelled the white man

"No, I won't go there because there is a sign that says, for whites only," responded the black man.

During our long, long drive to East London, there were many agricultural fields and mountains. The African tradition is that the family and the extended family live together in one house. As the family grows, so does the house. On the road through the Transkei Homeland Wild Coast, there are also many Rondavels (huts) where people sleep on the straw floor. Along our drive, goats stopped in the middle of the road to scratch. Zuks, called it a mobile stop sign.

There are nine Provences in South Africa:

Eastern Cape, Western, N.W. Provence, Free State, Ganteng, Northern Provence, Mpumalanga, Northern Cape and Zulu Natal

This is the land where an ATM machine is called "Auto Cash" and a take-out restaurant is called, "Take-away."

East London

After a long drive, we arrived in East London, Blacky's hometown. I resided at the Blue Lagoon hotel located on a hilltop overlooking the lagoon surrounded by lush homes and condos. The hotel has an outdoor pool in which to relax after a weary day of touring, a bar, and a deck next to the dining room.

During our tour of the city we visited City Hall. Just in front of the building Mandela had dedicated a statue of Steve Biko (1946-77), in his memory. Mandela and Biko were incarcerated at the same time. Unfortunately, Mr. Biko was killed while in prison on **Robben's Island**.

Cape Town—Miami's Sister City

From East London, we boarded a South African Airways plane destined for Capetown. From my window I saw voluminous mountains and the most generous stretch of coastline surrounding South Africa. Capetown is the Sister City to Miami. The population is three and a half million with 350,000 squatters.

Many years ago, European settlers opened wineries and they continue to flourish. I toured the palatial estate of the Spier Winery. The Dutch built this H shape house and decorated it with Dutch paintings, chinoise-oriental, Chippendale chairs and tables, and crystal chandeliers. It's also a place for fine dining on assorted dishes; I couldn't even taste everything because there were too many choices. The buffet cost only $18.30 US per person. We chose to dine on the verandah under a large umbrella, because the weather was perfect for sitting outdoors. There was a boutique that sells homemade products on the other end of the property. I was informed that there are plans to develop a hotel and recreational activities for the whole family.

After lunch, we attended a wine tasting. The lecturer informed us that grapes are harvested early in the morning. I also learned a little about wines, such as the different acidity. The black fume casks (barrel), is an aging process in order to produce superior wines. The tin Savion Blanc, allows the wine to quickly ferment. These techniques permit two distinctly different tastes and aromas. We were told that we should never throw away leftover wine. It can be used for cooking. I met several local people who invited me for a drink later. I figured, what could they do to me that hasn't been done already.

I resided at the Lord Charles, a five star hotel. It's a bit out of town, but a delightful property with oodles of amenities and a breathtaking view of the pool and the mountainside. There is a Scottish bar, dining by the pool, indoors formal dining, and a gazebo to stage a wedding, conference facilities and a ballroom. It's the little things that make a difference, such as when I entered my suite, on the screen of the television, "Welcome, Mr. J. Haggins" and a bottle of champagne with fresh fruit.

Lunch had been prearranged at the Grace Hotel on the Waterfront. It's a five star hotel with amenities such as: a box of biscuits and herbal teas of your choice and convenience. All of the suites overlook the harbor. It's within walking distance from everything one could need. Some of the best entrees and desserts were served, such as fresh local fish and a mixed fruit sorbet.

Later that evening, I met with the people who had invited me for a drink at the Alfred & Victoria Waterfront. The Waterfront is a very large commercial mall on the harbor with lots of shops and restaurants. They suggested that we have a drink in the Grace Hotel. I stated, "Oh, no, I had lunch there" so they chose another delicious spot. They were very informative of their town and invited me to call next time I come to town. When the evening was coming to a close, I asked their hotel concierge to call my concierge to bring the car around.

Following Mandela's Footsteps to Robben's Island

An early departure to board the first ferry to Robben's Island. We arrived at the dock at 8:30 a.m. The cost was $16.00 U.S. The weather was perfect for a tour of the island and as we departed, I had a clear view of the harbor and Tabletop Mountain. Robben's Island is a twenty-five minute modern ferry ride across the bay. I couldn't believe we were going to visit the prison on the island where Mandela was incarcerated for twenty-seven years as the leader of the ANC. As we left shore, an educational film on the history of Robben's Island appeared on the monitor in the cabin.

From various articles I had read, I imagined the island as a very depressing place to visit. As we approached the harbor, the island was green and fertile with several pastel colored houses. After we disembarked, we boarded a van and toured the island where gazelles and impalas roamed freely in the open range natural reserve. We stopped at a stone quarry where the prisoners used to chop stones. Working in the quarry caused blindness from the reflection of the hot sun against the stones. We also passed a graveyard for Lepers. Originally the island was used as a hospital/asylum for Leper victims. Lepers were sent and buried there, for fear that they would spread their disease. They were evicted in 1931. In the 1800's the island was used as an English prison. Then it became a defense Military Island from 1937-57. It was used as a maximum-security prison until 1996. The island has applied to UNESCO to be recognized as a national museum and nature sight.

The ANC men who were incarcerated with Mandela are now tour guides at the prison. I asked a guide if it was difficult to return to his old stomping grounds each day. He informed me that his options were limited. He didn't have a choice of employment because there is a forty- percent unemployment rate in the country. As we walked from one corridor to another listening to the inhumane conditions these men had suffered, I felt as if I was in West Africa, where many of our people were castrated. It takes a strong willed man or woman to come from all this despair to become the president of a country and promote forgiveness.

My first recollection of hearing Mandela's name was through his association with the ANC and his fight for equality and freedom for the Black's in South Africa. Here in the United States during the 1960's African/Americans were going through the same black power struggle. Blacks were in the majority in South Africa, yet unable to vote and share freedom with the rest of the country. Blacks were not even allowed to walk on the same sidewalk with the whites.

He pursued his dream, that someday all men would be free. However, he knew it was against the law to fight and contradict the white system. He was incarcerated for twenty-seven years on Robben's Island, a twenty-minute ferry ride off the coast of Cape Town. But what he wanted most for his country was to end the apartheid and free his black countrymen. In his heart he knew that all men should be free and treated equal.

I can't imagine having spent twenty-seven years sleeping in a small cell in a prison and chopping granite in the quarry under the bright sun day after day. However, he found time to read his books and write his autobiography, although the prison confiscated the first manuscript. Mandela never lost his perspective and steadfastly focused on his goal. When he returned from the abyss to civilian life in 1992, he wasn't bitter, he opened his heart and forgave, but will never forget his past. In 1994 his countrymen held him at high esteem and elevated him to the pinnacle of his life as the President of South Africa.

Before departing the island, I visited the local boutique, which is filled with memories of the island's history. There were postcard photos of the lighthouse, Mandela's cell, military buildings and the wildlife on the island.

Tourism is developing as a number one industry. To empower black South Africans is to provide a hospitality school for training. This will enable them to assume responsible positions in the hospitality industry.

South Africa is a very special place and I'm so proud of the people. Visiting South Africa, before Mandela retired was a dream come true. South Africa is the land of beauty, hope and dreams.

Brazil

Left: Man playing birimbau

Below: Folkloric dancer in Bahia

On the dance floor with folkloric dancers in Bahia

Chapter 8
Black Heritage in Brazil

Salvador

Salvador is in the state of Bahia and is only a two hours flight north of Rio along the coastline. Imagine the tropical blue waters of the Atlantic Ocean rushing to the shores of Brazil in the dead of our winter. The seasons are opposite of the United States. Then imagine being there and capturing the essence of Brazils' rich heritage. The flight to Rio de Janeiro, Brazil is only nine hours from JFK.

Portuguese is the national language and it is the language of love; so what if it sounds like steam heat. The currency is the Real and so are the people. Approximately one hundred and eighty-five Reales (R$) is equal approximately one US dollar.

Brazil is one of the countries that imported Africans as slaves to work the cocoa plantations in Bahia. It has the largest African/Brazilian population outside of Africa. In the heart of the city underneath Mercados Modelo, in the lower city are the slave dungeons. Listen to the influence of the hypnotic African drums in Bahia. Drums have influenced the rhythm of the world.

Salvador has a superb natural harbor; it was Brazil's first capital and major trading center under the Portuguese Empire. You'll find the roots of the Yoruba religion, which arrived with the Africans. Candomble and Umbunda (the Saint houses) are worshipped as powerful, capricious beings, each with its own constellation of attributes. The most important saint houses are the Axe Iya Nasso, Axe do Ops Afonja, Axe Iya Masse, Ile Morololaje, Bate Folka and Tumba Juncara. They are associated with natural phenomena, with colors, with occupations and with days of the week. The drumming and chanting help carry believers into a trance where they are taken over by the spirit of an Oxixa.

Bahia

The city of Bahia was built in two parts; the upper and the lower city; which can be reached by steep roads, trolley car or Elevador Lacerda (elevator). Pelourinho was originally residential and the lower city was commercial. The lower city is surrounded by a beautiful harbor filled with marine life and sailing. Pelourinho is also the core of this metropolis with its cobblestone streets, pastel colonial houses and hotels and some of the world's most beautiful churches, such as the Golden Sao Francisco. UNESCO has restored and declared Pelourinho Square as a national monument. During the colonization of Bahia, the Portuguese used the town square as a whipping post for slaves.

The narrow cobblestone streets have barely enough space for an automobile to pass, as there are restaurants with tables directly on the street. There are many restaurants, art galleries, a theatre, an African Museum and shops with Brazilian goodies and endless entertainment. Several restaurants have entertainment and dancing in the courtyards. The young and old dance together or solo. After departing Pelourinho we walked to the elevator that descended to the lower city. Just across the street was the Mercado Modelo. The market was filled with fresh fruits, meats, fish and clothing that I bargained for. But underneath that peaceful market is a huge dungeon that is barely lit. It had been a storage bend for slaves. For the few moments I spent down there, the fresh air was short and I began to sweat. It brought back memories of the slave castles in West Africa.

Bahia has the best people's carnival; everyone joins in with the samba bands or Samba schools. Rio is known for the Samba, but it's danced throughout the nation and the samba is in the blood of every Brazilian, regardless of color. Brazilians are multicultural extractions of African, European, Portuguese, Indian and Asian all mixed into one melting pot.

Bahia is known for its Capoeira dance. Capoeira is the traditional dance that was created by slaves to disguise their defense. The slave owners outlawed the use of their hands to fight, because they wanted to preserve them for harvesting the cocoa crop. Capoeira is a deviation martial art: it's a syncopated, handstand, quick cartwheel, twirling counterclockwise, intricate acrobatic dance. Musicians accompany the dancers with a pluck on the strings of their birimbau instruments.

The Bahiana women dress in crisp, white starched cotton and lace dresses with hoop bouffant skirts underneath to give them a billowy look. A colorful sash around the waist accents their dress. Their heads are wrapped with a twist of white cotton fabric. They also wear lots of colorful beads around their neck, similar to Carmen Miranda. But Carmen had more fruits, nuts and beads.

There are many outdoor cafes, art galleries, markets and historical Black Heritage tours. Much of the artistry is inspired from Africa. The national dishes are **Feijoada** (the Brazilian soul food), which is made of sautéed collard greens, white rice, tapioca flour, black beans, pork sausages and peppers, and the **Churrasco** dish, which is a barbecue skewer of fresh beef. Don't forget to top off your dinner with a caipirinha drink, which is concocted with rum mixed with sugar and lime juice. After several drinks, it's difficult to stand on your own feet.

Rio de Janeiro

New Year's Eve is a very special time of year in Rio de Janeiro. The Candomble worshippers gather on the beaches to pay homage to Yemanja. Everyone dresses in all white clothing and carries clusters of white flowers, rice and fruit to set afloat out to sea. These offerings are made to "Yemanja," the Goddess of the Sea. They believe that if the flowers are taken into the sea and not returned, their blessing will be realized. Brazilians believe the offering will bring hope, prosperity and good health for the New Year. Yemanja is the mother of most African spiritual entities. Yemanja is the Queen in a memorable feast at the Rio Vermelho district.

Carnival in Rio is designed for voyeurs. The audience sits in the Sambodrome to observe samba schools parade in outrageous, elaborate, festive costumes. The grand samba balls invite tourist to dress in costume or black tie and participate in the festivities.

Hot! Hot! Hot! As the temperature climbs, I suggest you wear the briefest bathing suit and relax on the lush beaches. There are many beaches such as Ipanema and Copacabana with tall, tan and young and lovelies. Brazilians are beautiful, sexy people. After all, they invented the floss bikini. The boulevards are lined with many outdoor cafes from where you can watch the tan, young lovelies sashay along the wavy, mosaic sidewalks. Brazilians are very passionate about life in general, soccer in particular. Maracana is the grand stadium, but soccer is also played on the beaches. I attended a game where unfortunately the Russians won 1 to 0 and the Brazilians were very upset. They tried to burn Maracana Stadium down.

For street wear, use your imagination and wear colorful, festive, tropical attire as the locals wear it. From the beaches you view the mountains, so take a cable car up to Christ the Redeemer who stands tall on top of Corcovado Mountain with a watchful eye over Sugar Loaf, the city and the harbor below. To get to Sugar Loaf Mountain, catch an aerial tram at Praia Vermelha. From a height of 394 meters, you'll be able to see the Guanabara Bay with the district of Botofogo and Flamingo. Westbound are beaches like Copacabana, Ipenema and Leblon. They can been seen with the hill known as Pedra de Gavea as a background.

Within a stone's throw across the bay is the island of Pakata. Motorcars are not allowed there, so you have the freedom of breathing unpolluted air. Bicycles are the only mode of transportation on the island. The houses are beautifully designed. Some remind me of Frank Lloyd Wright's designs.

Brazil is a fun, exciting and historical country to visit. I can describe my colorful experiences, but there is no way you can sense Brazil without being there. I fall in love all over again every time I visit Brazil.

Salvador, Bahia Is Magical

I invited the television crew from "GlobeTrotter Jon Haggins," to film a segment on Salvador, Bahia, Brazil. I wanted to share the culture, history, art, culinary, religion, dance and of course to lay on the sun drenched gorgeous beaches and watch the beautiful people go by. Brazilians have bodies that I would die for.

During my direct flight, I viewed an aurora borealis summer dusk sky from my window. I could see the midnight sun. It was like jewels in the sky (yellow, blue, green, red, orange and black purple blended into a watercolor sky). Just below I saw fields of lush fertile fields. Someone stated, "If you like history, Salvador is a magical place."

From the moment I exited the Vasp Airline jet, my heart was filled with joy and anticipation of visiting Bahia again. I remember the warmth of its friendly people who opened their hearts to me on my first visit thirty years ago. Salvador is a party town where the party never stops. The first word I learned was "Brigado" (which means, thank you). The people of any country appreciate it when you try to thank them in their native tongue. The Bahia Tourist office and Vasp Airline designed our tour. Several people on the flight enhanced our journey with updated information regarding Bahia. Bahia is a cultural and racial melting pot of the world (South American Indians, Africans, Europeans and Asians). As I carefully listened, a few familiar Portuguese words gained meaning.

The Catussaba Hotel, where we stayed, is a retreat away from the bustling city and a paradise for lovers. The hotel has all the amenities of a five star hotel: a designer swimming pool surrounding the cocktail bar that served the best caipirinahs. A caipirinah is a typical Brazilian cocktail made from Brazilian Rum, sugar and lime juice, poured over ice. Just for relaxing, there is a hammock on each terrace, a mini bar, and the Atlantic Ocean beach view. The dining room is an open verandah with palm trees. The property also has a tennis and volleyball court, a sauna and a fitness room.

During our tour of the city, we were introduced to Paula do Santos, a guide, who was extremely knowledgeable of the history of Bahia. The city tour familiarized us with some of the offerings of the city. I was amazed at how much the city had grown since my last visit. From a distance several designer colorful modern skyscrapers appeared as part of an art deco painting. One of the skyscrapers looks like an atrium of glass with a garden growing from each floor.

The coastline has beautiful honey and white sand beaches with swaying palm trees. The refreshing breeze of the tropical sea makes life bearable. While lying on the sand, I observed a small boy practicing capoeira, the national dance, with his father. I asked my crew to capture the moment. This was Brazil at its finest. Later that afternoon, a cluster of fishermen was reeling in a net with the catch of the day. Many of the traditions are maintained from Africa such as the way they throw the net from their dugouts. They do this twice daily. I stopped to observe a fisherman with a fish in his back pocket. The fish kept flipping as if the man had a tail attached to his body. After all the fish are sorted, they divide the catch.

The state of Bahia is equal to the size of France. Population is 12.5 million and 12 million are African or mixed. Eighty percent of the population is of African descent. The Africans refused to forget their traditions and culture of Candomble. We were invited to a Candomble ceremony where the women were dressed in the typical Bahiana billowy white cotton dress with their heads wrapped and tied into a turban. The drummers beat their drums while they sang and marched in a procession in a circle, calling on the spirits. A young man from a German television crew got the spirit and went into a trance. Someone had to brace his camera.

Just north of Salvador is the city of Cachoeira, the town of the sisterhood of the Good Death. Cachoeira is the second largest city after Salvador. It was once a wealthy port for sugar and cigar transports. The sisterhood is a religious order of women whose purpose is to maintain and pass along their African heritage to the younger generations. In order to join, one has to be at least sixty years of age. Members dress in freshly starched white cotton cloth with billowing crinolines underneath. Their heads are also wrapped. Their dress is accented with strands of beads, which indicate different regions. The Sisterhood of The Virgin of Good Death was started to free African Women. These ladies are the Priestesses of the African religion. Yoruba is another religion that was started 225 years ago in Brazil. August is the month of Boa Morte (good death). Everyone in this religious order dresses for the occasion and pray in the BonFim church.

Every state in Brazil except Bahia celebrates Yemanja on New Years' Eve. Bahia celebrated Yemanja on February 2nd. Yemanja is one of the eight Deities that Bahianas pay homage. She is the Goddess of the Sea and is represented in the form of a mermaid. For the celebration, Brazilians dress in white and walk into the sea and make offerings of white flowers and perfume into the sea to pay homage and give thanks to her. It is believed that if the offerings are taken out to sea, that prosperity, health and fortune will be granted.

The Banda Dida band of women drummers strike a hypnotic drumming sound as they march the cobblestone streets. Every Terca feira (Tuesday) the squares are filled with entertainment to entertain a lively crowd.

During my visit, the moon was full and smiling down on me every night. Although Capoeira is what Bahia is known for, they also samba. I finally learned to do the Samba; the secret is in the bending of the knees.

Roberto, the guide, introduced us to many restaurants where only the locals frequented. I enjoyed them because they were inexpensive and the food was delicious. Many of the restaurants served large portions that I divided with someone. Brahma Chopps light beer is the most refreshing chaser for any meal.

Sightseeing

One of the most amazing churches is Sao Francisco in the heart of Pelourinho. The interior is covered in gold leaf and pictures of saints. The missionaries converted slaves to Catholicism and had them design and build the churches in the mid 1800's. The majority of the Brazilians are Catholics and there are one hundred Catholic churches throughout the city.

The Barra Lighthouse was built in 1580's at all Saints Bay on the peninsula. Bonfim Church (Lord of Good Will) was constructed on the highest point of the city. A wealthy boat owner from Portugal was lost at sea during a storm. He prayed that if he was rescued he would build the most beautiful church at the highest point of the city so that people could come and worship.

Dique do Tororo Park is in the heart of the city. Placed in the center of the lake are eight Orixas, (Afro-Brazilian Deities) sculptures. They are the great gods and goddesses of protection. The Bahiana are very proud of their musical heritage—musicians such as Caetano Velosa, Joao Gilberto, Gilberto Gil and the hot rhythms of Olodum Band, who have recorded with Michael Jackson and Paul Simon.

The Bale da Folorico is an energetic, colorful dance company that opened its performance with an undistracted stare and a snap of the right hand starting from the forehead, then stomach, then right chest and finally the left chest. It was the gesture of the Catholic cross (Father, Son, and Holy Ghost, Amen). The forty-five minute production included a fire-eater with a flaming bowl in each hand and another on his head. The group danced to the lyrical voices of a women's chorus while the men were plucking the Birambou and beating the African drum. There were also sword fighters, bamboo sticks and manchete defense teams and capoeira dancers. Capoeira is an acrobatic cart-wheel-twirling dance that has to be synchronized to precision; otherwise someone gets hurt. There were also men and women in skimpy loincloth coverings paying homage to the fisherman. The show included Samba dancing and everything that represents Brazilian culture. The very next day I saw some of the same energetic smiling faced dancers dancing in the middle of the street. The Federal government sponsors the art programs to enhance the arts for tourism.

The drive from Bahia up the Green Line Coast took several hours, but it was well worth the time. We ventured to coastal city of Praia de Forte to see the best collection of large sea turtles in captivity. Garcia D'Avila Castle and Projeto Tamar are ecological organizations dedicated to the preservation of the sea turtles. The turtles are the size of a six-year-old. Of course there were also the ubiquitous souvenir shops.

Sampling the Local Delicacies

A short drive from Praia do Forte is Praia de Guarajuba. It's the best local beach with lots of regional foods including lobster, fresh fish, acaraje (deep fried corn meal, dende, hot sauce with shrimp) salad, vatapa (paste, dende, pepper liquid—really spicy), and moqueca, which is a fish stew, prepared with fish, shrimp, octopus, oysters and then stir-fried with palm oil and coconut milk. Usually accompanied by other African style dishes, such as Vatapa, caruru and farofa de dende and hot pepper sauce. The flour of the manioc root, a staple of the native Brazilian people is an important ingredient in many of their dishes. I bought some of the local coconut sweets sold by the Bahiana women on the street.

While I was having lunch on the beach, a nine-year-old boy approached me to buy his wares. I told him I wasn't interested. Then he asked if he could have the food that I wasn't eating. This inspired me to ask the other people from the crew to share their food. Suddenly, three boys appeared and devoured every bite. I also ordered sodas to wash their food down. They were forever grateful. As we were entering the car, they came to show their appreciation, "Obrigado." I reached into my pocket and retrieved some loose change, which made them very happy.

On another day, our driver maneuvered through the bustling traffic and arrived in the nick of time for us to board the yacht bound for the Island of Itaparica. From the minute I entered the yacht, the hypnotic pulse of the African/Brazilian drum began to liven up the enthusiastic crowd of Latins from Argentina, Uruguay and other lands. Everyone was in a party mode and I felt romance in the air. One young man from Argentina didn't have a clue about rhythm. He stood on the bow and danced like a loose monkey while everyone laughed. I danced the Samba with a lady from Argentina. The dance wore both of us out. The schooner crew offered fresh fruit to whet our appetites for their special caipirinhas. After partying for an hour and a half, we docked at the Island of Frades (Monk Island) for a short stop over to explore. There was a church on top of a mountain and a lovely beach with a shopping market for tourists.

We continued our sail to the Island of Itaparica. Most of the guests were lifted to shore by a launch. I chose to wade in the water. As we maneuvered to shore, we were greeted with a grand reception of Bahiana women dressed in the traditional dress. Lunch was a buffet of assorted dishes, fruits and desserts. The temperature was hot and a cold Brahma Chopp beer was the order of the moment. During and after lunch, a young group of capoeiera dancers performed. We took a short bus tour of the island to a medicinal mineral water spring. The stretch of beach was covered with white sand, as are most beaches in Brazil.

There are thirty-six islands off the coast of Salvador. On our return to Salvador, I observed the magical skyline. It reminded me of a view of Manhattan's Riverside Drive with its metropolis of skyscrapers.

Carnival is a very exciting time when folk come from far and near to share in the festivities, which last for seven days starting on a Wednesday night and ending the morning of Ash Wednesday. Bahia has the world's largest party and everyone is in the streets to celebrate and participate. Some dress in costumes. There is music everywhere. Some join Carnival clubs to parade and sway behind their favorite musicians.

Each night as I returned to the hotel, I reflected on the daily activities. The best part was having a caipirinha in hand, lying on a chaise next to the pool or swaying in my hammock on my terrace while looking up at a full moon. The moon beamed through clouds and the stars appeared to be turned on one by one. The nights were still; the only sound I could hear were the waves splashing against the shore. It's a very romantic place, even if you're alone. I opened my French doors onto the terrace overlooking the verandah, the pool and the jardin, and I took long early morning walks along the never-ending beach to reflect on the different experiences I had encountered. Bahia is a party town and it has the rhythm of life. I can't wait to return.

A Cultural Experience in Rio

Rio always rings a romantic notion in my ear. I had last visited Rio in the early 1970's and experienced one of the most exhilarating times of my life. I was looking forward to returning to the land of dreams. From the moment I checked in and boarded Varig Airlines, I felt the warmth of the Brazilian Cariocas. I almost danced the Samba down the aisles. The flight attendants were surprised I spoke a few words of Portuguese. The flight offered several dinner selections; pasta, chicken or beef and a delectable desert.

The Portuguese founded Rio in 1565 as a port city to transport their products of sugar cane, coffee and gold. Gold was transported to Lisbon, Portugal. The city was named Rio de Janeiro (January River) because the Portuguese discovered it in January and thought the bays were rivers. Most people think of Rio as just Copacabana and Ipenema, but it's much more than that. However the Copacabana Palace Hotel, a five-star hotel, built on Avenida Atlantica in 1923, is still one of Rio's grand guest residents. I stayed at the Le Meridian Copacabana, a four star property just down the avenue from the Copacabana Palace. Le Meridian's buffet introduced me to luscious tropical fruit and a large selection of assorted salad and hot dishes. What I loved most was the warm and friendly "bon dias" (hello) welcome I received every place I visited. The view from my suite was breathtaking with a sweeping panoramic aerial expanse of Christ the Redeemer standing tall on Corcovado Mountain with a watchful eye over the waterfront.

There are two stages on the cable car to Sugar Loaf Mountain. The cable car was built 1908-1912. As we floated effortlessly up the side of the mountain in the cable car, I felt as if I was flying through space.

Another afternoon, we took a trolley car up Corcovado Mountain to visit Christ the Redeemer. While waiting for the trolley to arrive, a Pateca (badminton birdie with feathers) merchant and a partner played the game, then invited tourists to get involved. After a few bats, I bought several and quickly turned a fifty- percent profit by selling them to other tourists. The ride up the side of the mountain was quite an experience of height and wonder. I don't know if the Redeemer is considered one of the wonders of the world, but it should be. The Catholic Church raised the money for the construction of the Christ and it was designed and built 1926-31 by Hector da Silva Costa. The French constructed the head and arms.

On yet another afternoon, I felt as if I was on top of the world, circling in the helicopter around the Christ the Redeemer and the city's landscape. Four years ago, the helicopter sightseeing tour was established to fly to different destinations above the city. The cost ranges from $43.00 to $148.00 U.S., with a maximum of ten passengers per helicopter.

One cannot go to Rio without visiting the H. Stern and Amsterdam Sauer gem stores. They are located next to each other on every block. The majority of the semi precious stones are found in Columbia, Brazil, Zambia and Zimbabwe. Stones with names like Tourmaline, Topaz, Rubettite, Aquamarine, Topaz and Emeralds. Brazil is known for its Emeralds. I was informed that the darker the emerald, the better. Emeralds are never perfect; there is always some degree of imperfection in the stone. Most of the mining is executed in Minas Gerais, north of Rio. Volcanic rock, pressure and heat create the stones. Stern's has a permanent semi precious stone collection in the main store.

Soccer is the national pastime and the passion of the Brazilian people. I found everyone playing futubal (as it is commonly called) on the beach. The professional games are held in Manacana Stadium with a capacity of 100,000. Brazil is a four-time World Cup winner 1958, 1962, 1970 and 1994.

I visited Garota Ipenema Restaurant for a typical Churrasco Misto no Recheaud (barbecue) dinner at $13.00 U.S. including steak, sausage, chicken, pork and rice. It's a traditional stop for a "chopp" (beer) after the beach. One of the most popular dishes is Mandioca (a root vegetable tapioca). This is the very restaurant where Antonio Jobim and Vinicius de

Moraes wrote, "The Girl From Ipenema," in the 60's. Helo Pinheiro inspired the song. It's still one of the local hangouts with a bustling crowd. There are memorabilia items lining the walls. This is only a small sampling of what Rio has to offer.

Rio is more than a Beach

Most people think of Rio as a destination to go lay back and enjoy the beach. Rio has many cultural things to offer. One of Brazil's icons, Carmen Miranda, has a museum containing many of her costumes, jewelry and photographs on display from her Hollywood years in the 1940's. I visited another Brazilian priceless treasure, the Sao Bento Monastery. It dates back to mid 1522 and was finished in 1641. Among the artistic heritages there are woodcarvings designed by Frei Domingos da Conceicao and executed by Alexandre Machado, works by Mestre Valentim, and paintings by Frei Ricardo do Pilar and Jose de Oliveira Rosa.

When I first visited Rio, the Municipal Theater was used for the big, formal, carnival ball. Now it's used only as a theatre for operas and classical performances. It was designed and built by A. Guilbert and Francisco de Oliveira Passos and inaugurated on July 14, 1909. The main murals are by Eliseu Visconti. Just across the street is the National Library. A neoclassic style building that is surrounded by Corinthian columns, it was inaugurated in 1910. The collections began to be formed in 1530 and prominent features are two copies of the Mainz Psal'ter, a book printed in 1462 by Gutenberg followers.

Many of the downtown Colonial buildings have been refurbished and it's very active during the day and evenings. I had lunch at the Colombo Coffeehouse. This magnificent continental café has changed little since opening in 1894 and retains an air of restful elegance. The cooking is at best competent, and at worst, you can argue that the dishes have been left standing since 1894.

Largo Do Boticario is located on the other side of town. It's a courtyard with seven colorful town houses that form one of the most enchanting locations in Rio de Janeiro. It's a very special atmosphere that was enhanced with colonial facades, cobblestones streets and ancient trees.

I was driven out to Suburban Rio where we passed construction of condos and homes. Through the winding hills we landed at The Bira de Guaratiba restaurant, which is perched on the side of the mountain overlooking the sea. The owner insured fresh seafood because he caught it himself. I was told that people come from far and near to devour his special recipes. Fauna that surrounds the restaurant, gives it a mysterious and romantic setting. Several monkeys climbed down from the trees to accept the bananas being offered by the restaurant guests. This was a spectacular day out in the unspoiled beachfront with only the sound of the birds and the bees.

More to See

Later that day, we visited Casa Do Pontal Museum of Brazilian Popular Art. The museum houses what is probably the best and most complete collection of the country's popular folk art. There is a collection of over 4,500 pieces that belong to a French man, Jacques Van de Beuque. He has been collecting Brazilian artifacts for over forty-five years since he arrived in Brazil in 1946.

We also toured Roberto Burle Marx Park. It was the home of world-famous landscape designer Roberto Burle Marx from 1949 through 1994. This estate covers 350,000 square meters, with thousands of plant species ranging from the rare lacquer palm from Malaysia to Brazil's famous ironwood. On the property, there is a waterfall, a church and his home, which contains modern tapestry pieces. I also discovered that he designed the middle lane of the walkways along Rio's beach.

If anyone ever says, "Get out of Town," I suggest taking a tour of Tijuca Forest. It's the largest National Park in the world. As you look up at Corcovado from the Lagoa (Lagoon), the mass of greenery you see clinging to the edge of the mountain is the Tijuca National Park. Roads run through the entire length of the park allowing visitors to enjoy its many natural wonders. There are all kinds of activities such as hang-gliding and biking off the side of the mountain.

One afternoon we attended a Maccumba (Condomble) session. Condomble is a religious order that was brought over from Africa many years ago. Brazilians pray to the deities for prosperity. As the ladies paraded around the room in a circle, I felt as if they were acting, not genuine. I had seen Candomble in Bahia and I felt it was the real thing there. Even with the beating of the drums, I slept.

Just on the other side of town is a national park and Chacara do Ceu Museum, which was once the home of collector Castro Maya, there is a permanent collection of modern art (Portinari, Picasso, Salvador Dali, etc.) as well as furniture and decorative items.

Another tour included Ruin Park. There is a magnificent view over the picturesque Santa Teresa district with the city at its feet. This park houses the remains of the mansion that was once home to Laurinda Santos Lobo, a leading hostess who was one of the mainstays of social and cultural life in Rio from the 1920's until her death in 1946. Today, reflecting the cultural life that once flourished there, this park features an exhibition hall and auditorium seating 100, with a horizontal window offering a postcard view of the Sugar Loaf.

After touring Ruin Park, I hopped on a trolley down to the Cathedral. The Cathedral is built in a cylindrical shape with the highest ceiling and decorated with expansive stained glass windows.

The Hippie Fair is held in a park in Ipanema every Sunday, where I ran up and down the aisles grabbing everything I could get my hands on. There are artsy-craftsy items throughout the market and across the street, a grocery store to purchase coffee and nuts.

Our final dinner was held in Rodrigo de Freitas Lagoon's kiosk (Tom Jobim Park). The park is the best-equipped park in the city of Rio. The silhouette of the Tijuca massif, dominated by the peak of Corcovado, Dois Irmaos Hill and Gavea Rock, form backdrops for its striking setting alongside the lake. Jobim Park is a favorite spot for sports enthusiasts of all types: walkers, joggers, bikers, and those who enjoy paddleboats. The area has food kiosks, playground equipment, gym bars, bike paths, a skating rink, an amphitheater, soccer fields and parking lots.

Living Like the Locals

I wanted to do what the Cariocas do. So I asked to go to a typical place where I would only see Brazilians. Café das Artes was perfect because there was live Brazilian music and a lively crowd that invited me to Samba. I surprised several people because they didn't know that I knew how to Samba.

Rio is not Rio without a Carnival. The Mangueira Samba School allowed tourists to have lunch (Feijoada) while watching and participating in their rehearsal. I danced with one of the hoochie, coochie girls with a string up you know where. The samba is an exhilarating dance that everyone must do, while in Brazil.

Uruguay

Casa Pueblo in Uruguay

Below: Salvo Palace, Montevideo

On horseback at San Pedro de Timoto Ranch in Florida, Uruguay

Local musician in Montevideo

Chapter 9
Uruguay the Land of Dreams

Small Country with a Big Heart

Uruguay is a small, South American country, crushed between the bosom of Brazil and Argentina. As we drifted through the voluminous clouds, from my window I witnessed a lazy, hazy morning. Descending, there were bright beams from the sun reflecting off rooftops like diamonds on a tiara and shimmering on the water of the Atlantic Ocean. It is a twenty five-minute flight on United Airlines from Buenos Aires, Argentina to Montevideo, Uruguay.

Amy Ucar from the Uruguay Tourist Office and Mario (the driver) met me at the Carrasco International Airport in Montevideo, and greeted me with a warm welcome smile and an embrace. I felt very much at home. They shared their country with pride, humor and a warm personal touch. They even remained calm when I lost my return airplane ticket. Fortunately they were able to secure another ticket.

Uruguay encompasses nineteen states and is located in the warmest sub-region of South American's southern temperature area. It's the second smallest South American country next to Ecuador. The total population is approximately three million. Six percent of the population is of African descendent. The official language is Spanish, but French, English and

Italian are also spoken. The peso is the unit of currency and approximately 9.71 pesos equals $1.00 US.

I stayed at the Victoria Plaza Hotel, in front of Independence Square. The hotel has lush suites with all the amenities, indoor swimming pool, gym, sauna, conference halls, casino and a breakfast penthouse dining room overlooking the harbor. After checking in, I casually walked out of the hotel swinging my camera through the Puerta de la Cuidadela (door of the city). The gate of the city is the remainder of a wall that used to surround the city to stop the Portuguese expansion towards the (*Rio de la Plata*) river Plates. Thus its role as a strong bastion of the Spanish Crown.

While walking through the old city, a very nice middle-aged man warned me to guard my camera. I had no fear and his guard was a little dramatic. After all, I'm from New York City. There are many open-air bistros in the squares with large umbrellas shading the tables. I quietly sat and ordered a chivito (typical sandwich), which consist of chicken, egg, tomatoes, mayonnaise and lettuce with a side of french fries. At first I thought…an egg in a chicken sandwich? It was delicious. I also ordered a chopito (small) local beer (Patricia). It had a little bite and was refreshing on a hot afternoon.

Standing tall in Independence Square is a very large statue of Jose Gervasoi Artigas. He led the country to independence on August 25, 1825. Unfortunately, he died in Paraguay in 1850. The first constitution was signed in 1830 and the first president, General Fructuoso Rivera, was elected. Diagonally across the plaza is the old Salvo Palace, which was built in 1925.

Montevideo—Many Personalities

Montevideo is a very dramatic city with many personalities. One evening, I visited Baar Fun-Fun, an old bar and restaurant where Tango singers perform. The walls were filled with memorabilia and photos. Behind the bar was a latch door refrigerator. This is a very popular local hang out for those who have a passion for Tango. I recommended it to several Germans that I had met on the plane. When they returned home, they e-mailed to tell me they had their best evening at Fun-Fun. The singers were very dramatic with their gestures. They sang with gusto and rendered the songs with the feeling of an aria. At the end of each song, I screamed, "Bravo...Poppy" or "Brava Mommy." Amy and Carlos found humor in my enthusiasm. They also told me I was unusually friendly by greeting everyone with "buenos tardes" (good afternoon), "buenos dias" (good day), or "buenos noches" (good night). I stood before an audience and blurted, "Buenos noches Dames y Caballeros?" I was puzzled because everyone laughed. I quizzed, "What happened? What's going on?" "Do you know what you said," Amy asked. "No," I replied. "You said, 'Good evening ladies and horses.' But you should have said, "Buenos noches Dames y Caballeros."

We drove up to an old military fort on top of a mountain. During summer months, there is a cable car ride to the top. At the top, I found a souvenir shop with lots of goodies and a restaurant with an aerial view of the harbor. Cascading down the mountain was a radio tower and another fort to ward off the enemies of the past.

After descending, we rode through the Prado section where the first aristocrats lived. Many of the original mansions still stand. In a small park is a sculpture by Jose Ballone. It's a very important stagecoach sculpture of a gaucho transporting leather, meat and other animal products to the market from the farms.

Some of the country's traditions:

▼ Medio y medio—white wine/champagne. A wonderful cocktail.

▼ Chorizo al pan—sausage with bread. A quick sandwich

▼ Cantar Musicals ambulantes—singers perform around the city in full regalia from restaurant to restaurant.

Uruguay is a very romantic place. I can imagine bringing a loved one or a special person and falling in love again and again. There are miles and miles of endless beaches stretched along the southern coastline parallel to the boulevard of the city.

The city of Montevideo has two golf courses: Cerro Golf Club and Punta Cerretas Golf Club. A long stretch of coastal beach surrounds the city and allows everyone to just sit back and enjoy the rush of waves or jog along the cornice. Or pass time sitting in a bistro in a square in the old city.

We met with Mr. Benito Stern, the Minister of Tourism, to discuss the economic health of the country. He informed me that Uruguay is the second largest user per capita of the Internet in the world. They export meat, wool, rice, milk, and dairy products as well as leather. Like Argentina, they are known for their beef. Chemical processing, meat and fish processing and oil refineries are among the industries found in Uruguay.

The first slaves arrived in Montevideo Harbor in 1743. They were servants. Then Brazilian slaves settled on the border during the revolution of 1846. Ships escaping Brazil brought them. Blacks were used as soldiers; many died from yellow fever.

I met with Beatriz Ramerez and Juan from Mundo Afro (a woman's help group). Their organization is ten years old and publishes a newsletter to update their members and promote black awareness and education. The black community in Uruguay consists of 164,000. Mundo Afro receives institutional support from Evangeliste Church and has obtained a low interest loan from the state and federal government for housing. The organization is encouraging young women who drop out after Junior High to continue their education so they can have a competitive edge in the job market. The country has false integration.

It was a long, scenic drive through the rolling hills and fertile fauna from the capital city of Montevideo, to the northeast state of Florida where the San Pedro de Timote Ranch is located. We made a pit stop to stretch our legs and share a chopito (small) cerveza (beer). On the road, we passed several groups of gauchos herding cows and sheep. Gauchos are known to be free-spirited. Generally they never marry, but they have a girl friend and a bunch of dogs.

An Estancia Adventure

As we arrived at the ranch, it appeared to be a small Spanish town. Entering the gate of this fascinating place opens up a new world of Uruguay's history. The proprietors, Jose Pedro Cerisola and wife, Sylvia Feliciano, welcomed us with a smile, a giant sized hug and a kiss on the cheek. They bought the ranch two and a half years ago and have taken pain in restoring it to its original splendor. The ranch encompasses a rambling oasis of 2,600 acres.

150

Estancias (cattle ranches) have become a tourist attraction because everyone is invited to participate in the chores of herding or feeding the cattle or just laying back and enjoying the peaceful existence of nothing but the big open fields and a clear sky. It instilled images of the old Western movies I saw as a child.

There are thirty beautifully furnished suites. My suite contained an incredible French armoire made from a Jacaranda tree. The verandah was filled with rattan furniture, pillowed with English chintz and a slowly propelled ceiling fan. Alberto Gallinal built several ranches at the end of the last century. And this is one of the most beautiful. It is self contained with a church; fix it shop; guest houses with thirty suites; a hydro massage room with anti-stress therapies, massages, chromo-therapie, phyto-therapie; treatment center; main building; video and historical book library; tennis and paddle courts; game room with a pool and ping-pong table. There are also three meeting and convention centers, two outdoor pools and a heated indoor pool. In front of the dining hall is a playground with wooden sculptured animal for the children. There are several corals with cows and horses. They even have a private airfield.

On the first afternoon, everyone mounted a horse for a ride into the open fields. This was my first time on a horse, so one of the gauchos assisted me. I sat planted firmly on an English saddle and projected confidence, although I was petrified. When I inquired as to why one of the guests wasn't riding, he stated, "I'm too fat." "Did the horse tell you that?" So he decided to ride in the wagon with the surrey fringe top, which was pulled by a tractor. I offered visual directions to my horse by holding the rein and pointing with my index finger, "Go that way, horsey." The horse didn't move and the other participants had disappeared into the horizon. I just didn't know how to get him to move. Later someone explained that the horse only speaks Spanish. They instructed me to tap the horse on its side with my heel in order to request it to move. Suddenly, the horse began to gallop. Well...I was not prepared for his fast pace. I demanded, "Whoooa, horsey," but to no avail. As we approached a small ditch, I pleaded, "Please don't drop me in the mud."

Suddenly, it began to rain and I wanted to return to the ranch, but "Oatmeal," as I called him, only circled the same perimeter. I called him, Oatmeal, cause he was so slow. There were sixty acres of trees creating an escape from the blazing sun, which didn't happen to be shining that day. I was very impressed with the vastness of the land. It was an oasis away from reality. As we rode further into the land, I turned my head in search of the ranch, but it was nowhere in sight. I only saw trees, grass and several dogs following the herd of horses. Then I wondered if I'd ever see the ranch again. Suddenly, we exited the brambles, the ranch appeared, and I rejoiced. Upon stepping off my horse, I removed my left foot from the stirrup and then my right. But unfortunately, I stepped off on the left and slid under the horse for an unbelievable plop to the ground. Carlos Ferriera, one of the gauchos, rushed to my aid for fear that I had broken my back. Fortunately, I was intact!

Every afternoon at five, there is a call for teatime, which consists of tea, coffee, biscuits and cakes. It's a perfect time to sit around the bar or dining room, chat about the events of the day, and get familiar with other guests. One of the guests shared her pineapple and vanilla birthday cake with other guests.

Uruguayans eat lots of barbecued Parillilla (Pa-ril-ya)—assorted meats: steaks, ribs, intestine of the cow, blood sausage, mild sausage and chicken. The barbecue is cooked over a wood flame, which gives the meat a different flavor. There was also a combination of assorted salads from vegetables from the garden on the ranch. Everyone drinks mate (ma-tay) an herbal tea that helps with the digestion. I had a little Russian vodka with Paso de Los Tores Aqua Tonica. Amy ordered a Pepsi Quella (Pepsi Cola). Christine entertained us with several traditional Uruguayan songs while strumming a guitar. The fireplace added warmth to the dining room. It erased the damp coldness of the rain of the early evening. It's a very romantic place to be with a very special person.

After dinner, we ventured out in the surrey wagon for a night drive. We saw sheep, deer, armadillo, beaver and a rabbit.

Breakfast consisted of coffee, tea, juice, fresh yogurt, croissants, bread, cakes, fruit salad and prunes. After breakfast there were rides into the wilds to start the day. By now, I'm an old cowboy (or gaucho) who's in full control of the rein. I mounted my horse and patiently waited until the other guests had mounted; then I led the pack.

San Pedro is implanted in my memory as a fantasy come true. It was the highlight of my trip.

Punta Del Este

Amy Ucar and Roberto were great conversationalists and shared Uruguay with great pride. I was told that Punta del Este was a "must see" during my short visit. It became a favorite south shore destination in 1940 after the town of Piriapolis was suddenly a bit passe for the newly rich. Punta del Esta is the Beverly Hills of Uruguay. There are many large "Architectural Digest" designer homes surrounded by lush acres of fertile fauna. One of the weekend homes did not fit into the scope of my camera lens, it was grander than a mid size hotel.

The town has its own airport for private jets. The view is of huge ocean waves crashing to the shore. A short hop and a skip on the ferry across the waters is the island of Gorriti which contains the largest botanical collection in the country and is one of most important in South America.

The town has a large craft market on Gorlero Ave (the main boulevard) that offers leather, wool items, wood, gems and silver. I spent hours walking the aisles for their specialty items. I visited several hotels to check out their accommodations.

In the Punta Ballena area (point of the whale) the Casa Pueblo is a unique hotel built on the side of a cliff overlooking the sea. Famous artist, Carlos Paez Vilaro, who maintains a wing of the hotel for his personal use, designed it. The hotel has a modern day caveman's feeling with all the five-star amenities. The hotel is a very popular destination for locals and foreigners. It offers time-shares as well as regular hotel accommodations.

The city has many gambling casinos owned by the government. But the Hilton Hotel has the only independent casino. San Rafael Hotel is built in

English Tudor style and is the second largest hotel after the Hilton. Uruguay has one of the worlds' largest collections of vintage cars (calchilas) and a convention of vintage car owners stays at the hotel for the weekend car show. Old cars are treasured in Uruguay and are often used in movies and international car shows.

Las Dunas Hotel located on the beach is a very romantic spot for lovers. Getting there is an adventure because of riding across the La Barra Bridge (dip bridge). It's the most unusual bridge—you feel as if you're on a roller coaster, going up and down as the road dictates. Many of the large private homes in this quiet residential neighborhood in Punta del Esta have well-manicured lawns with the name of the houses posted on the front lawn to identify mailing address. Within the neighborhood is a golf club that Robert Trent (a noted golfer) had designed.

Soccer by the Seaside

In Piriapolis, a seaside resort, is the Argentina Hotel, built 1920-1930. It took Francisco Piria (who built the town) ten years to build the hotel. It's an enormous hotel that faces the sea and looks like a huge European palace from the past. On the streets of Piriapolis, I witnessed the excitement of Uruguay winning a soccer game against Brazil. Everyone emerged onto the streets screaming, laughing and blowing their horns and whistles. I hadn't seen this much excitement since I was in Manacana Stadium in Rio.

My favorite was the Hotel L'Auberge. It's a dream hotel with theme wall coverings in each suite and French furniture, Jacuzzi® etc. Several rooms are offered in the tower with aerial views. The junior suites start at $240.00 per night and there are thirty-six rooms and a golf course quietly by the sea.

As I had asked several locals for destinations that I should see, they recommended the Belle Mont Hotel where Prince Charles, Liza Minnelli and Hillary Clinton have stayed. I figure, if it's good enough for them, then it's good enough for me. The boutique hotel has thirty-eight rooms in the Carrasco neighborhood.

I spent several nights at the Hotel La Capella (chapel hotel) in Punta del Este in a quiet residential neighborhood next to a church. The hotel has an open court with an outdoor swimming pool and lush fauna.

I shall always remember Amy and Carlos because they are very special friends. They called me Santa Claus, because of my boisterous laugh. I love to laugh and suggest packing a sense of humor wherever you travel.

Ecuador

Parade in Quito, Ecuador

Left: Musician in Quito

Below: Juggler in the old city, Quito

Chapter 10
Ecuador—Cosmopolitan
Cities in Ecuador

Ecuador is located on the northeast coast of South America, on the equator, the center of the world. The country possesses many layers of rich history, culture and music. Continental Airlines flies from Newark to Ecuador in eight hours, including the forty-five minute stop over in Panama City. The flight attendants served baked chicken, mixed vegetables, seasoned rice, salad, cheese and chocolate moose for dinner. The early morning breakfast was scrambled eggs, fresh fruit, juice, yogurt, a roll and jam and coffee or tea. I always drink lots of liquids when I fly to prevent becoming dehydrated.

We landed at Simon Bolivar International Airport in the city of Guayaquil. The city of Guayaquil has a population of 2 million, while Quito has 1.5 million. It only takes thirty-minutes by plane from Guayaquil to Quito. General Bolivar helped liberate five Latin countries, Peru, Columbia, Bolivia, Ecuador and Venezuela from Spain. Juan Jose Sucres declared independence for Bolivia, Ecuador and Columbia from Spain in 1822. Ecuador's population is 12,500,000 with 2,600,000 living in Guayaquil. The altitude of the city is 8,200 meters

The currency is Sucres and approximately 15,000 Sucres equals one U.S. dollar. I overnighted at the Oro Verde Hotel (green gold). My favorite breakfast juice was Maracuya or passion fruit. I felt especially tropical as it slithered down my throat.

157

Paulina Morena and Gasby Salgado from Canodros Tours greeted me in Quito and ushered me to the Sebastian Hotel. The Sebastian Hotel is located in the modern section of town. Room rates start at $25.00 U.S. per night. They provide great accommodations and cuisine. The surroundings are quiet and the suites are nicely furnished. My room had a seaman's chest. The furniture was masculine, yet comfortable for a woman. There are several bistros within a short walking distance from the hotel. I wore a light jacket and sweater for my brisk walk, because it had rained earlier that evening and the air was damp. I stopped at one of the bistros for a Club beer (national brand).

Public transportation is readily available and plentiful. There is a modern trolley system with stations in the middle of the highway. Lots of buses roam the streets. The most distinguished part of town is the old section; it has the best collection of baroque architecture and the Spaniards built colonial churches during the fifteenth century. Each church was grander and more elaborate than the last one built. Missionaries came in and converted the Indians to Catholicism and that is the dominant religion of Ecuador. Seven Crosses Street has seven churches. Conception Church is at Cathedral Independent Square; El Sagrerio has a gold interior. Principle Square was designed in baroque colonial while occupied by Spain; the San Francisco church there also has a gold leaf interior. Spain built many churches, raped Ecuador of its gold, and other natural resources, and gave little in return. But now the city seems protected by The Virgin Mary (Virgen de Quito), who stands high above the city on a hill.

Quito is a bustling metropolis with many town squares where people busily parade through the streets with generous smiles on their faces. There are also many markets with offerings of pork rinds, table dressings, fruits and vegetables, balloons, household products, eyeglasses etc. There were many street performers juggling balls in the air or stilt walkers to charm the children. I also witnessed a parade of colorful people from different provinces. Groups of folkloric artists display their paintings every Saturday in the park.

I spent two nights at the Swissotel, which has all the amenities. There was an indoor and outdoor swimming pool, gym, three different restaurants, a bar, and a gambling casino, where I dropped my change. I was very fortunate to be there at that time as the Ecuadorians and Peruvians were celebrating the Peace Treaty between the two countries. Alberto Fujymori, the President of Peru, visited our hotel during my stay and there was lots of fuss regarding his appearance. Each night, a Peruvian band played in the bar and restaurant. I was fascinated with one of the instruments; I asked what was it. "The jaw of a goat," a musician replied. As he struck it, it rattled and vibrated with a gogogogong sound. I had never seen anything like it before.

I always wondered what it would be like standing on top of the world at the equator. Paulina drove me to the Monument marking that line. I thought there would be a plaque designating the equator, but instead, there was a formal monument of grand scale that was constructed in 1986. At the entrance to the park is an avenue of busts of 13 men who made expeditions to Ecuador during the 1700's, two Ecuadorians; nine French and two Spaniards. The 'Media del Mundo," (middle of the world) is a nine-story monument with an elevator that brought me to the top for an aerial view of the city which is surrounded by mountains. Walking down the stairs through the museum, I viewed a wonderful collection of the country's history and its twenty-three provinces, including costumes, instruments, basket-weaving display etc. I also saw a goat jaw instrument on display, identical to the one used by the Peruvian band at the hotel. The complex has incorporated a village of boutiques and restaurants to relax in. I bought several T-shirts for friends and a mohair sweater for $20.00 for myself. One building housed a miniature model of the city designed and directed by Guido Falcony. His model city demonstrated the transition of day into evening as the lights of the city turned on. Passing over the city was an effect of clouds and the sound of thunder. I asked if he could make it rain. He responded, "The model is made from cardboard. What do you think?"

Ecuador manufactures all the Panama Hats that everyone thinks come from Panama. I wanted to purchase one, but it didn't look right on me. A short walk from my hotel was a folkloric shop with all kinds of souvenirs. A short distance away is the Cultural Center. The Colonial doorway was incorporated in the new architecture. The gallery exhibits, modern paintings, drawings and sculpture. The Cultural Center is a modern annex to the Universidad Politecnica Seleriana.

I was told that Esmeralda Province, in Ecuador, has an African population of approximately 35,000. Although I didn't personally explore it, because there just wasn't enough time. Hopefully on my next visit, I will go north to the coast to visit Esmeralda and witness their culture for myself.

An Ecological Lodge at the Basin of the Amazon

The Amazon has veins that wiggle their way like a spiraling ribbon. As I was flying over the arms of the Pastaza River that flows into the basin of the Amazon, there were miles and miles of monochromatic green trees with an occasional yellow color popping out. The jungle appeared to race like a jaguar against our single engine Cessna Gran Caravan, twelve-passenger plane. The clouds stood still like Easter Bunnies suspended in the sky, while the jungle raced by. The vastness of the Amazon and its denseness reminded me of a huge tapestry of green broccoli standing tall. There are inter-weavings of thatched roof villages along the river and Anacondas waiting for a snack.

Kapawi is in the most remote area of the Ecuadorian Amazon Basin and is accessible only by small aircraft. We landed at Wayusentsa, a short dirt airstrip, where if I had yawned, we would have missed it. At the end of the strip, is a quick drop to the river. At the other end of the strip, was a family of Achuar Indians, waiting to greet us and offer us a welcome fruit drink. Our luggage was dispersed from the plane as we were quenching our thirst. The weather was hot; I stripped to my undershirt. I asked a local for direction to the men's room. He pointed to the left, then the right and finally behind him. He meant I could go, wherever I wished.

Until the early 1970's, the Achuar were the last indigenous group in the Ecuadorian rain forest that had remained isolated for centuries. With age-old traditions still intact, their land has remained untouched by logging or oil companies. The Chachis Indians construct dugouts, weave baskets from tree bark, weave thatch roofs and cloth. Many Achuar Indians work within the lodge and operate the riverboats. Handicrafts of bowls, combs, and weavings are sold to the lodge for their tourist boutique.

We descended on a steep, wood plank, stairwell that led us to the riverbank to embark on a dugout that transported us one and half-hours down the river to the Kapawi Ecological Lodge. The palm trees stand proud, tall and graceful. The jungle has over a hundred varieties of trees and plants. Long winding vines with budding flowers hung over and in the river. There were many shades of leaves from crystal to forest green. A strange green worm landed on my pants' leg and scared me half to death. The only sounds on the river were the birds and the boat rumbling through the swells. There was a trickle of water and the sweet sound of birds leaping from one branch to another. There are actually three hundred and forty-three species of birds and a large variety of assorted yellow, orange, white, blue and green colored butterflies fluttering their wings.

The lodge was built to help preserve the natural environment of the Rain Forest. Kapawi is a five-year-old project owned by Canodros S.A., a privately held corporation. Canodros formed an agreement and partnership with the Achuar Indians to train them and operate the lodge. The project took two years to build and has been operating for three. Canodos invested two million dollars in this project. In 2011, after fifteen years, the Achuar Indians will take possession of this project without any investment.

The facilities include a private bath with each cabin, deck with chairs and a hammock overlooking the lagoon, a terrific lookout point for bird watching, twin beds, kitchen and dining room, boutique, library, bar and family room to share stories of the day's adventures. There are twenty double rooms with a sun-heated shower and electricity provided by a photovoltaic system. After a full day of conversation and adventure, everyone retired early, because breakfast was called at 6:30 a.m. Every guest pays a ten-dollar land use tax before departing.

The only means of communication is a high frequency radio. There are no phones, no cell phones or television to distract from the tranquil environment. The shimmering sunset silhouetted the trees against the aura borealis sky. The water was calm and lonely; everything was still and somber with an occasional tweet and coooo. During the evenings, we ventured out with a flashlight in search of crocodiles. Shining the light into their eyes paralyzed them. During our search, I saw two Bacabemonite or Grandbesestias, an endangered mammal wading along the shore. They reminded me of hogs. Turtles were resting on the riverbank to lay their eggs. I blurted out, "Who wants to take a night walk? Uh, Uh, say no!" I also spotted Bromeliadis – red blooming birds of paradise from the pineapple family. The leaves were glistening in the sun and growing in the midst of the jungle were guava trees with clusters of white flowers with yellow and red bellies.

Water from a spring flowed into the river, spilling off from the rain. The floral fragrance of the jungle and fresh air was tranquil and refreshing. Everything was at peace. Even the dead trees lay in harmony in the river. I saw many Guayacus trees (strong wood for building). They bear yellow flowers.

In an Amazon village, Takamash is the male side of the hut. It's also the family room where guests are greeted and treated to a bowl of Chicha (beer). The Ekent is the female side with a bed and lots of pots and pans. Intimate activity is performed in the jungle, not in the house. The woman goes into the jungle to give birth and the male has nothing to do with the birth of the child.

The lodge offers walking tours through the jungle and bird watching expeditions along the river. The Kapawi bird looks like a small turkey. Walking through the jungle is definitely a tranquil experience. There was only the sound of the patter of our feet and various birds and jungle sounds. A bird called out and I mocked him with a repeated echo whistle of his sound.

Doors to the cabins are never locked in the camp. I felt free and relaxed. This was a jungle experience I will never forget.

Preserving the Ecological Galapagos

The Galapagos Islands are approximately 400 miles off the coast of Ecuador in the Pacific. I had always imagined the Galapagos as a very special place with lots of untamed sea life roaming throughout the islands. I landed on the island of Santa Cristobal, one of the four inhabited islands of the total thirteen islands.

We cruised the islands on the Explorer II, a five star, three hundred-foot ship, with all the amenities and a staff that granted my requests. The ship had a library, pool, sauna, game room, gym, dining room, several bars and a piano player. There are fifty spacious cabins, including two large suites with a terrace for honeymoon couples to gaze up at the evening stars. All cabins had great views of the Pacific Ocean. This particular cruise was shared with a group of fifty cardiologists from all over South America and several from the United States. They were truly party people; they danced and sang and closed the bar every night.

This is a perfect cruise for water lovers. There was a choice of snorkeling, scuba diving and swimming. Naturally the launch was available to bring everyone to shore. I witnessed an array of dolphins leaping out of the sea into acrobatic dives. There were birds diving into the water to retrieve a fish dinner.

At our first landing, we climbed to Point a Pitte with Philippe Degel, who is the foremost naturalist in the Southern Hemisphere. I witnessed goats observing us from the top of the mountain. Philippe lectured on the eco-logical environment and how they are protecting it. The goat population is approximately 80,000. They are vegetarians and climb to find food. The vegetation growing on the mountainsides reminded me of a patch-work wool sweater.

After the 1930's, government legislation protects parts of the Archipelago. Galapagos National Park has its present boundaries and it stands for the preservation of sea and bird life. I walked on soft lava rocks inside a crater while sea lions lay on the soft white sand beach. The male guarded his turf by making loud calls to warn others to stay off his territory. The mother sea lion protected her young from predators on the beach.

Each day we docked in another port and boarded the dinghy to take us to explore the islands. We visited Espanola, Floreana and Santa Cruz. There were lots of sea mammals, birds, sea crabs, colorful Iguanas and sea and land Turtles on view. Turtles come ashore to lay three eggs in the same spot each year, but only the first-born survives, because the infants are attacked by predators.

Charles Darwin National Park and Natural Habitat on Elizabella Island had a collection of turtles of all sizes and ages. There was also unusual cactus, mangrove trees and of course Lonesome George, an eighty-year-old turtle that weighs five hundred and fifty pounds. I don't know why he's called lonesome because he has so many females around.

Everyone was excited about the Boobie Bird with their blue feet and the Albatross with their long beaks. They looked like ducks with big feet. Late in the day we visited an eclipse of a blowhole, where the ocean rushed into shore, burst into this hole and exploded into the air like a firebomb. The bird life took all of this so casually.

We alternated between wet and dry landings. Santa Cruz was a dry land-ing. I thought we had landed on the same island as the previous night. I was puzzled for a few minutes, because after a while, all the islands began to look alike. They shared one common thread, lots of souvenir shops for the tourist to drop their last buck. Tourism is the number one industry in the Galapagos.

While I was in this glorious environment, time didn't seem to matter. The attitude was very laid back and there was never a rush for anything.

Fiji

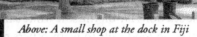

Above: A small shop at the dock in Fiji

Left: Local musician

Below: Comparing muscles with Fiji man

Jon paddling away from ship in Fiji

Chapter 11
The Exotic Islands of Fiji

We landed at the international airport on the island of Nadi, Fiji, an island in the South Pacific Ocean. Air Pacific sort of coasted to its landing without a single bump. I was greeted after an early morning arrival with a grand pearlie white "Bula" (welcome or hello). As I was retrieving my luggage, I noticed some of the Fijian men were wearing Sulus (wrapped skirts). I quickly whipped out my camera and started photographing them. The Fijians are a combination of Africans, Indians and indigenous people with a population of 75, 000. The majority is of African decent. The U.S. dollar equals approximately $1.85 Fijian.

We were transferred to the Tanoa International Hotel and rushed in for a buffet breakfast of tropical fruits, French toast, sausages, bacon, boiled eggs, etc. The thatch walkways shaded me from the sun as I walked to my room. Unfortunately, there wasn't enough time to splash in the outdoor pool at the hotel.

After breakfast, we headed out for a day cruise, sailing around the islands on the SeaSpray yacht. Just before arriving at the dock, we passed through a well-manicured golf course, which is the property of the Sheraton Royal Denarau Hotel. The SeaSpray is an eighty-three foot two-mast schooner (of television fame). It's a seventy-five year old sailing vessel that has been completely restored. That beautiful vessel took us exploring through the crystal clear waters, beautiful beaches and lagoons of the Mananuca islands. There are one hundred dialects and three hundred islands. Baun is the general language.

I met a honeymoon couple Okatani and Osmu on board; they had just married on September 4th, one day before my birthday. We explored uninhabited beaches and islands and stopped off to snorkel, swim and visit a traditional Fijian Island village. In every village, there is a market where one can shop for local crafts such as sea shells strung together into a necklace or bracelet, palm leaf hand fans and grass skirts, unusually designed conch shells and beautifully tie-dyed subus. A Kava ceremony gathered locals to meet with us and allowed us to drink Kava, the traditional drink that tastes like mud. We also stopped at Monoriki Island where the movie "Castaway" staring Tom Hanks was filmed. The island also has a Castaway Resort.

Within minutes, everyone put on snorkel gear and dived in the warm, lapis and turquoise Pacific waters with large white diamond swells for as far as one could see. I was next to last to dive in. However I didn't realize that our yacht was moored approximately 1,000 feet out. I began to swim and approximately halfway in, I realized my endurance was depleted. As the other swimmers passed and left me far behind, I begged one swimmer to wait for me. I knew I was in serious trouble being that I am not a strong swimmer. But I was determined to reach shore, no matter what. I finally huffed and puffed and reached the shore, then looked out to sea and thought to myself, "They have got to send the launch to retrieve me; there is no way I will tackle the return." There was nothing on this tiny island except wind blown swaying palm trees, white clean beaches and a few seashells. After a leisurely afternoon, I strolled along the beach and sat along the shore to reflect on how absolutely, magnificent and wonderfully, unspoiled the Fijian islands are. A launch was sent to retrieve me and lunch was prepared on board.

Several of the crew played and sang typical Fijian songs. John played guitar and bass, Jacob and Iliesa played ukulele and Captain Jone serenaded us with both instruments. Fresh mackerel was grilled on the deck – it had crisp outer layer with a moist and delectable inside. My mouth moistened for each morsel that crossed my lips. The chef also included steaks and sausage with pasta, rice, garden salad and fresh tropical fruit such as papayas, oranges, pineapples and watermelon. There was lots of champagne, beer and soda to cool off with.

After lunch, I was a bit jet lagged and decided to lay back and enjoy the sun rays being brushed against my face by the wind. Within minutes, I had fallen into a restful nap, breathing nothing but fresh Fijian air. As we sailed into the wild blue yonder without a care in the world, I thought to myself, why can't life be like this every day?

That evening, we shared dinner at the Fiji Mocambo Hotel in Nadi. The chef had prepared a special menu of Fijian dishes, including prawn soup, fresh fish and steak with vegetables and rice. We were given a Frangipani flower to place in our hair. Wearing it on the left means you're looking for romance and on the right means you're taken. I was too exhausted to eat the cheesecake offering, so I retired to the lobby to wait for everyone to finish. At the end of the evening, I walked along the property, which is filled with tropical floral gardens. At each hotel there is always a recreational pool to splash in and a chaise to lounge on.

Early one Sunday morning, we attended a church service at the Koroitamana church. The men wore a Sulu and a jacket with a white shirt and a tie. Ladies wore white dresses or floral prints landing just below the knee. The locals embraced us for our interest in visiting their church. The first prayer was in English to welcome us into their house of worship and the second prayer was in Fijian. There were two choirs, one adult with four-part harmony and the other a group of young voices that sang like angels. The adult choir was harmoniously uplifting and exhilarating. After the service, we were asked to form a receiving line at the front door. Every member of the church shook our hand and personally welcomed us as they exited the church. I was elated and felt that I had died and gone to heaven.

A Luxury Cruise in the Fiji Islands

The Blue Lagoon MV Mystique Princess Cruise is a one hundred and eighty five-foot yacht that departs twice a week on Sundays and Wednesdays at 3 p.m. The itinerary includes a visit to Mananuca and Yasawa Islands. There are thirty-six, air-conditioned staterooms, a one hundred-twenty seat dining saloon, air-conditioned forward lounge, foyer, boutique, three sun decks, two cocktail bars, Purser's Office and aft boarding platform. As I approached the boarding platform, Captain Ieli, dressed in his white officer's uniform with stripes on the his shoulders, greeted the guests with a big Bula, Bula (hello).

As a member of the crew brought my bags into my cabin, I was reminded that I had left my valuables in the safe back at the hotel. No problem! The captain summoned a member of the crew to retrieve them, so that when I disembarked, they would be waiting for my attention.

As we departed from Lautoka City Port and motored out to sea for a three-night cruise, we were chasing the electrifying turquoise water with white diamond swells as they rushed against the shore from island to island. The coastline on either side of the lagoon or Pacific Ocean displayed many islands that appeared to be rising out of the sea. Special uninhabited islands with white sand beaches and swaying palm trees helped to paint an impressionist picture of the tropics. On this windy afternoon, the leaves appeared to be brushed in the wind like a woman with long hair.

The first night, we anchored south of Naviti Island with a welcome champagne drink on the sky deck at sunset hosted by Passenger Services Director Fasiu. The crew joined in for some local music, which was followed by dinner hosted by Captain Ieli and officers in the Dining Saloon.

Next morning at 6 a.m. was the start of the early morning swim. Well, fuhgetaboutit. I only wanted to know my pillow at that time of morning. Of the twenty-five guests, only four signed up for an early wake-up. The first water taxi to shore for swimming, snorkeling, or just lying on the beach was at 9 a.m. Morning tea or coffee was served on shore. Brief snorkel lessons to brush up and then everyone dashed out to the reef. We returned to the boat to depart for Liku Beach activities of swimming, snorkeling etc. Some folks chose the hill walk to lose a pound. When I arrived at the top of the hill, the aerial view of the ship, sea and the island was breathtaking.

After mustering up a little anxiety, a barbecue lunch was prepared on the beach. The Fijians have an expression, "The more you eat, the better you float!" After lunch we rejoined the ship and sailed to Nacula Island to visit the Novotua Village for a traditional dance ceremony and Kava. Everyone danced and drank Kava and soaked in the atmosphere of a Fijian Village. The villages have extended families and everyone shares their wealth. The women of the village set up their shell market following the Meke or cultural dancing. Kava (Yaquona) is a ceremonial drink made from the root of a pepper tree (piper mystheticum). The root is at least five years old when matured and first sun dried before been pounded in a steel mortar. The powder is infused in water for the resulting mix, which is non-alcoholic and mild. It is supposed to help you relax. We were instructed to clap once before and three times after we drink, then say Bula! to the host. I was anointed Chief of my group and led them into a thatched roof recreational facility. Everyone had to walk behind the Chief. As Chief, I had to sample the Kava first. It tastes like gray mud. When offered another bowl,

I raised my hand like a stop sign and yelled, "No more please!" After a prayer, we were invited to dance with the locals in a symbolic tribal dance. The local performed an energetic, coordinated dance with arms and legs going in every direction. None of the tourists could follow suit.

Fifteen years ago, the Blue Lagoon Cruises purchased fifty acres of the beautiful Nanuya Lailai Island from Burns Philip Shipping and now it becomes my private 'neck of the woods' for a day and night. This is our private island – to swim, fish feed, sunbathe, etc. There are toilet facilities, spy boards and paddleboats available on shore, and a bar. The glass bottom boat fascinated me. It seemed to bring the tropical fish within fingertip reach.

Dinner was Lovo on the beach. Lovo is a cooking method adopted around the Pacific from Hawaii to New Zealand. It is essentially steam cooking, with heat supplied by pre-heated river stones. With no salt, seasoning or oil added in the preparation of the Lovo, the pig, chicken and beef is cooked in its own juices, and presents a unique taste that is hard to resist. More Kava was served. Some folks got a kick out of devouring it. After dinner, there was an international competition for the best singer, dancer, comic or poet.

Every morning there was an early swim or snorkel that I fortunately missed. The final morning, we set sail back to Lautoka City Port with breakfast in route. Finally, the crew gathered and sang a farewell song before we arrived in the port. The trip was relaxing.

We had to get a little last minute shopping in, so we taxied into Nadi for items to bring to friends and souvenirs for ourselves. Downtown Nadi is dense with shops and good manners. There were no traffic lights, yet cars stopped as a courtesy to the pedestrian.

After all the cruising and touring we relaxed at the First Landing Hotel. The hotel is located on the sea overlooking other islands. The property has a collection of bures (bungalows) with screened porches and thatched roofs. Kokoda, one of Fiji's most famous dishes was served for lunch. Walu marinated with fresh lemon, onion, tomatoes, red and green capsicum (peppers), coconut cream and a touch of chili wrapped in a banana leaf. That was a big laugh for everyone. The grounds include a bar for socializing, lush gardens, gazebos for dining or a wedding and an ocean front view. What more can you ask for?

This was the most exotic, romantic experience of my life. Vinaka (thank you).

Puerto Rico

Left: El Junque Rain Forest

Dancers at Jazz Festival

Left: El Morro Fort

El Conquistador Hotel,
Puerto Rico

Chapter 12
Adventures in Puerto Rico

Discovering the Cobblestone Streets of Old San Juan

After a three and a half-hour American Airlines flight, I landed in Puerto Rico (which means the rich port). I hired a taxi to transport me to the San Juan Grand Hotel in Isla Verde, just a hop and skip from the airport. The hotel offers lots of amenities such as a VIP lounge on the 15th and main floor, a large pool with a cascading waterfall, and an outdoor pool bar next to the beach. The long stretch of beach and skyscraper hotels reminded me of Miami Beach. The Atlantic Ocean's tropical turquoise water was warm and relaxing. I walked miles before it got too deep.

First night out, I walked the lonely streets, but never felt alone because of the warm generous smiles of the people. Puerto Rico is a people's island. I had dinner at the Parrot Club Restaurant. It's one of the hottest spots for people watching and fine dining. The sound of Eddie Wakes, a cabaret singer was reminiscent of Nat King Cole except when he scatted; then his style reminded me of Al Jarreau. The cuisine was elaborately displayed. The appetizers were a collection of spare ribs in Tamarinda sauce, fried calamari, chicharrones (small chicken parts with rice), thin plantain stripes, yuca-potatoe chips, salsa-mango and honey sauce and olive oil.

Puerto Rico has only two kinds of weather—hot or rainy. The streets are made of blue cobblestones that were imported from Spain. The winding streets are lined with fashionable boutiques and trendy restaurants and bars with only enough room for one car to pass at a time. I saw a haber-dashery shop with straw Stetson hats that are typical of the island. The streets remind me of the attitude of the people, happy and tropical.

Each time I visit Old San Juan I feel the essence in time gone by, with its Colonial architecture and the friendly attitude of the people. Old San Juan has so much vitality; you have to witness it.

I toured the El Morro Fort surrounded by the Atlantic Ocean and the San Juan Bay. It was built between 1540 and 1783 to keep seaborne enemies out of San Juan. El Morro features a maze of secret access tunnels, dungeons and a museum. The fort was used as a look out point and to protect the city from the enemy. El Morro has been designated as a National Historic Site and part of a World Heritage Site administered by the U.S. National Park Service.

In search of the "World's Smallest Bar," in Old San Juan, I stopped in Maria's Restaurant and Bar anwas told that the owner had died two years ago. And after his death, they closed the bar. It truly was the smallest bar in the world.

Dinner at Amedeus included sweet potatoes sliced like potato chips. I can never get my fill of Old San Juan; there are always new surprises.

After a short taxi ride to Condado, I found the best soup I've ever tasted in a restaurant at the Condado Hotel. It was lobster bisque with an empanada dropped in the middle. It was puréed and delicious. I asked the chef for his recipe, but he wouldn't part with it.

I used to visit Puerto Rico every month until 14 or 15 years ago. Some folks actually thought I lived there. On each visit, I would dine in La Mallaoquina Restaurant. The restaurant is decorated with linen covered dining chairs, slow, propelled ceiling fans, mahogany-framed mirrors, oriental vases, etc. The food was always good and the atmosphere delightful. I felt that if I didn't stop in La Mallaoquina, I didn't feel as if I was in Puerto Rico.

The coastline has all kinds of activities such as cruises, flea markets, street performers and tourists taking pictures. A must see is the Convento Hotel. Originally it was a convent for the sisters, but now it's a stylish hotel with fancy boutiques and cafes, located in the heart of Old San Juan. San Juan is the first capital of Puerto Rico, and it's a capital place to visit.

Adventures in Puerto Rico

I arrived early at the Rio Camuy Park and met with Freddie, Jose and Roberto, the tour guides for the adventure of my life. I never imagined descending 400 feet into the abyss. My stomach immediately knotted. I thought this was going to be an impossible task. It had rained early that day and the sides of the mountain were slippery and muddy. I had trepidation and seriously thought, how the hell am I going to survive this journey? Freddie walked our group up a slippery, muddy hillside to give us an aerial view of the Cathedral Cave into the abyss. The Cathedral sinkhole had just opened to the public. The guides can manage a group of fifteen for each tour. There are a maximum of two tours per day.

Rappelling was scary, thrilling and exhilarating as I was suspended over the great black sinkhole. My body banged and clanged on my way down into the sinkhole. As we began to descend with the help of several knotted ropes, I slipped in to the mud several times. Thank God, I wore long pants, unlike the rest of the crowd. I was frightened to death as I descended; I thought my life was over. After several slips, I managed to get to a flat surface to sit on a rock and rest my nerves. The gear included a helmet with a flashlight and a harness that looked like an over sized jock-strap with some sort of metal contraption called a carabiner, to anchor the rope while rappelling. Everyone was rappelling by request. I began to think that perhaps I'd made the biggest mistake of my life by agreeing to tackle this adventure. I wanted to return to the entrance point. I looked up and wondered how the hell was I going to get out of this mess. I was afraid because my sneakers didn't have a grip. I should have worn army boots with traction soles.

I needed lots of courage; I felt like the lion in the Wizard of Oz, as I sat on that big black rock and pondered whether I really, really wanted to do this. I asked myself, "Why am I doing this? I didn't have to prove anything to anyone." Then I focused on deep breathing, something I learned in Yoga and prayed that I would survive this outrageous journey rappelling into the abyss of the big black sinkhole. Everyone below egged me on, until I finally drummed up enough courage and got hooked up for the descent. Actually, I had never heard the term 'rappel' before. While dangling there, I realized the strength in my arms. Fear brings out surprises like that. The guides were attentive and gave me confidence and a "yes I can do it attitude." Once on solid ground again, I realized it wasn't as bad or dangerous as I thought. My basic problem was that I didn't wear the proper shoes. I needed serious army boots.

My constant concern was how we were going to get out of there. Hopefully, not the same as we entered. There was no elevator so I had reason for concern. I looked as if I had been in a mud fight and was not the winner. There are three other caves that are much less challenging and kinder to the less adventurous. A trolley brings one into the other caves and there are no ropes.

The trick to rappelling is to separate your legs and lean back. The position didn't seem natural to me, I kept forcing my body toward the mountain and that caused me to slip. As I reached the edge, someone yelled, "you're doing fine," as I banged into the stone wall and bumped my hip and elbow. Loose rocks bounced from my body and fell 250 feet into the cave. Another person suggested that I shouldn't look down. And that's exactly what I did. They told me to release my hands, I didn't understand and continued to feed the rope into the device at my waist. Suddenly my speed increased. I was rappelling at a dangerously rapid speed backward. As my speed increased, the friction from the ropes and the metal device heated up and I was forced to let go. Suddenly I landed in the arms of one of the guides. And thank God that was over.

As we explored the cave, we viewed painting the native Indians had crafted many years before. I continued to search for a way out, some sign of daylight.

I thought a cave was something I could just walk into from the street. I had no idea it was below the earth. Inside the cave, I was climbing and slipping up and down little hills of wet mud. After a forty five-minute walk, which seemed like forever, I saw the light of day. It seemed like a mirage. I quickly exited, slipping and sliding through green undergrowth and mud. I anchored my feet on top of rocks and tree roots to prevent further slipping.

The rules were one at a time down the knotted rope. I thought, perhaps I could meet everyone when they returned. They told me they would exit from another passage and that frightened me because I was left alone with nowhere to go. After we exited, there were several ropes still to climb. Later someone explained there that we climbed the same ropes earlier in the day. At the end, everyone was black and blue from the slips and bumps.

After this experience, I planted my feet firmly on the soil and thanked God I had survived. I had never heard of rappelling and never thought about climbing anything. On another trip, I climbed Dunnen River Falls in Jamaica and thought that was scary. It was minor compared to this experience. However, once I forgot about the aches and pains, I was delighted that I had shared this unforgettable experience.

When I returned to the hotel all muddy, the doorman wanted nothing to do with me. Every muscle in my body ached so I soaked my body in Epsom salts to soothe away the pain.

Another adventure was in El Yunque Caribbean National Forest. It is the only U.S. rain forest within the National Forest System. Well this was baby stuff compared to what I had experienced in Rio Camuy Park. Lush green fauna with an occasional budding flower, lots of climbing both ascending and descending and campgrounds placed sporadically throughout the park. Wind from the east meets humidity from the west and creates constant instant light showers. The park collects and receives 100 million gallons of water per year and park encompasses 28,000 acres with 240 tree species. Edwin Velazquez, the Forest Ranger, was very informative about the park and the history of the forest. Along the stone walkways were signs and plaques describing the forest and its fauna. There are several natural cascading waterfalls throughout the park along the walkways. I was told I could drink the fresh spring water and wouldn't get sick. The water drifted down to a reservoir to supply part of the city.

The El Conquistador Resort Hotel, a luxury property, is located outside of San Juan on 500 acres, which include three golf courses, spa, and three outdoor swimming pools. It also has a cable car that descends to the lower level of the hotel on the waterfront where I boarded a ferry that shuttled me to Palomino Island for a day of water sports action. The island is owned by the hotel and features jet skiing, water skiing, wind surfing, scuba and horseback riding along the balmy tropical water of the Atlantic Ocean. I just lounged and relaxed on the beach.

Heineken Jazz/Fest Jazz in Puerto Rico

Puerto Rico was hot! hot! hot! with voluminous Jazz vibrations filling the air. Heineken sponsors the Jazz/Fest annually. The festival was held in Sixto Escobar Park; located between Old San Juan and Condado. As I entered the press section, I asked a photographer, seated in the front row, if the unoccupied seats were taken. He responded, "They are for photographers." I quickly whipped out my Mickey Mouse camera and asked, "What do you think this is?" He laughed. Later, as I approached the stage to snap a few pictures, a guard confronted me and stated, "This area is reserved for photographers." "What, what?" I repeatedly asked. Finally he threw his arms into the air and said, "Fuhgetaboutit."

I seated myself in the second row and shared an extraordinary view of the stage and of the old Normandy Hotel. The Normandy is constructed in the design of a ship and appeared as if the Titanic had gone aground. I turned to observe the audience; it was a mix of locals and neighboring islanders with a sprinkling of Americans. Puerto Rico is not well known for its Jazz/Fest, but it's making an effort to broaden its horizon. Many internationally known jazz musicians performed during the four nights of the Fest. They came from far and near; Brazil, United States and the Caribbean.

The Rippingtons is a popular group that played Latin jazz led by Russ Freeman on guitar and backed by Dave Hooper, drums, Kim Stone, bass, Dave Kochanski, keyboard, Ray Yslas, percussion and Paul Taylor on sax. Eliane Elias trio from Brazil played romantic Brazilian jazz. She led the trio on piano and was complimented by Mark Johnson on bass and Satoshi Takeishi on drums. I closed my eyes and the mood of the romantic Brazilian jazz placed me at the top of Cocorvado mountaintop peering over the coastline of Ipanema.

The line up for the program included The Manhattan Transfer, a very stylish singing jazz combo. The anticipation and sheer thought of seeing a New York group away from home was very stimulating. Unfortunately it rained in Puerto Rico the night of their scheduled performance and the concert was cancelled. I was very disappointed.

Some of my favorite sounds were from Art Blakey's Jazz Messengers playing free style improvisational and carefree. The group of six musicians played "A night in Tunisia," one of Art's favorite pieces. The hypnotic sound of drums transfixed and transported my imagination to Tunisia. The heartbeat of Africa called out in the sound of drums.

My favorite instrument is the chekere, a calabash draped with beads that vibrate to create a rustic sound from the villages of Africa. The Latin groups were the pulse of Puerto Rico. Poncho Sanchez played an unbelievable syncopated Afro-Brazilian sound combining with the Guiro (sort of bamboo with ridges carved in and a flat piece of wood to rub over the ridges to create a sound). The Latin sound is so energetic and vibrant; it makes you want to get up and dance.

The night that rained out The Manhattan Transfer's performance, I attended a Pablo Casals symphony performance in the Casals' auditorium. The crowd was totally different. Actually they were dressed to the nines with their noses in the air. The best part for me was listening to the children's choir as they sang a cappella with their yet undeveloped voices. The orchestra appeared to be experimenting with sounds, instead of a symphony concert that I'm used to hearing. One of the musicians was distracting as he dashed across the stage clanging on different instruments and cowbells. It certainly was an original touch. Usually several musicians are hired for the various instruments.

The other thing I enjoyed most at the jazz concert was watching the reaction on the people's faces; their enthusiasm and appreciation for the music. Some of those jazz aficionados reappeared each night to soak in the essence of what jazz is all about. Fortunately, jazz is not limited to one country. America has been the jazz capital of the world, but I think jazz has a broader scope because every country contributes a nuance that helps to make it something special. The temperature and enthusiasm was perfect on a clear star studded night with just melodic jazz chords in the air.

Puerto Rico is an Island with lots of unforgettable personalities that have to be experienced.

Turks and Caicos

Vista of the sea on Middle Turk Island

Resort on Provo Island

Infinity pool at Parrot Cay Hotel

Chapter 13
Turks and Caicos

The Turks and Caicos Islands are located in the Atlantic, northeast of the Dominican Republic and east of Cuba. Turks and Caicos is a commonwealth of Britain. Everyone drives on the left side of the road. There are three major Islands in the Turks & Caicos group: Provenciales (tourist island), Grand Turk and Middle Turk. Grand Turk is the capital.

If you like ocean water and warm weather as I do, you'll love this paradise. There are white powder sand beaches and trade winds with a year round temperature of 85 degrees. The islands are known for their sea life. They are a haven for scuba divers. It's the king of destinations – where there isn't much you're compelled to do, and yet there are lots of options to keep everyone who feels the need of activity interested. When I was there, the water had the crystal colors of tanzanite, amethyst and aquamarine. Jewel-like tones glistened on the sea with a touch of white diamond swells rushing to the shore.

When I arrived on American Airlines at the Provenciales airport, I asked, "What is your favorite, typical dish?" "Grits," they replied. Grits are a part of our Southern breakfast heritage. They are served with eggs and bacon or sausage. Grits, for those of you who don't know, look like cream of wheat; made from corn. Africans brought southern recipes to the islands during the era of slavery. Conch fritters are another local delicacy. They also prepare a delicious cerviche conch salad with onions, pepper, vinegar and lemons. Rum punch is a refreshing drink at any time of day. Each island claims to have the best rum. I'm not a connoisseur; if it's wet, it's good.

I stayed at Beaches, an all-inclusive resort. The mere idea of not having to go into my pocket to pay for something was refreshing. Beaches is located on an irresistible stretch of beach. The property has many amenities for children and families. Most of the families never venture off the grounds. I was amazed at how many different facilities there are for children: video games, play rooms and an indoor and outdoor amusement park. If a family comes with a tot, there are nannies, to give the parents a little break.

I had an elegant dinner at the Anacoana Restaurant at the Grace Bay Club. I was surrounded by a twelve-mile beachfront view and a quiet dinner band playing tropical music under a star lit sky.

The city of Provo is continuing to develop more resorts and condominiums. Back in the 1970's, before the development began, local property owners sold their beachfront property for the price of an automobile. However, they are a lot smarter today. On the island of Grand Turk, which is unspoiled and underdeveloped, the locals are holding on to their property in order not to allow the developers to do the same to them. The architecture is Bermuda style and UNESCO has preserved the island as a historical site. I felt very relaxed on the island of Grand Turk because it's so peaceful and tranquil. It's only six miles long and one-and-a-half miles wide. It's also the capital of the islands. The oldest house on the island is the Turkshead Hotel, where I relaxed with a tropical fantasy drink, which was a concoction of several brews and fruit juice.

The National Museum on Grand Turks sits on a cornice overlooking the sea. There are fossils of old shipwrecks, samples of found treasures, and an aquarium of colorful tropical fish. There are lectures on the islands and about the history of their conquerors.

I took an all day excursion on the Silver Deep boat to Middle Caicos. The island is an oasis in the middle of the Atlantic Ocean. One of the highlights was visiting Parrot Cay Hotel, a very private, five-star resort on its own island. It's perched on top of a hill overlooking the sea. There is a landing strip for private jets. It's a hideaway for celebrities. There are sumptuous private villas, with two bedrooms, three baths, kitchen, deck, private pool and entrance to the lush beach. The central pool is an infinity pool that appears as if it floats over the sea. The deck is lined with wooden chaise lounges and large, white, rectangular parasols to shade delicate skin from the sun.

The islands inspired me to enjoy the five-day weekend and to relax. There are many water sports to participate in such as snorkeling, diving for conch, and viewing sea life below. Gibbs Cay Island is an isolated island with white sand beaches and not much else to do. There are many sting-rays along the edge of the beach; it was like Stingray City. I was told that they are people friendly and available to pet. Several approached me in the shallow water; I stumbled backward several times before touching solid ground on the shore. I was afraid. Actually, I don't like anything to touch me while I'm in the ocean, not even sea salad or weeds. I was told the stingrays are quite harmless, but I don't take chances. Someone yelled, "FISH." I jumped out of the water and ran ashore. One of the other tour-ists got her leg sucked by one of the critters as she was petting another. Perhaps it became jealous and wanted a little action too.

On the Middle Turks Island, I visited an enormous cave that had many entrances and exits. It was a haven for bats. I yelled out as I entered the cave. The cave was extremely dark, moist and slippery, so I used a flash-light to illuminate my next step. At one point, the ledge was so narrow I was sure I would loose my balance and topple below. The last straw was having to cross a narrow plank of wood, while placing one foot tightly in front of the other. I felt like a tightrope walker. In one of the cavernous areas, there were several black smoke spots covering the ceiling. The smoke covered ceiling was proof that the indigenous Indians held tribal ceremonies and ignited fires to provide light. There were also black water holes that had endless darkness. As I walked further, the ceiling became lower and I began to feel claustrophobic. I had an urgent desire to exit as quickly as I could. After going around in what seemed like circles, I finally recognized an exit and did exactly that. The other tourists stumbled fur-ther into the cave searching for bats; it's not what I needed to make my day. I waited outside next to the exit in the hot sun with a cold drink in hand and waited for everyone to return to share his or her bat experience.

After touring the caves, we visited the Blue Lagoon motel, a modest property, on top of the hillside, overlooking the aquamarine sea and white sand beaches. It reminded me of some remote destination from a travel brochure. The motel contained individual villas for guests to relax after a full day of snorkeling or diving.

On Little Water Cay Island, the National Park Association has established a sanctuary and natural reserve for Iguanas. In Manhattan, I'm afraid of a Chihuahua. Then I'm thrust onto the island and surrounded by an assorted collection of iguanas that walked slowly around my feet. There are wooden plank trails along the island extending from the beach. I surprised myself because I wasn't afraid of the little critters.

Once back on Provo Island, we visited the Provo Golf Club for lunch. It had rained earlier, but the sun reappeared and the course was radiant. During the rain, I was afraid that we weren't going to be able to share the Minx Trimirand excursion along the coast with the captain, Michael and Kathi Robertson. But after boarding and settling down, the captain pulled out of the slip and off we sailed, sharing nautical tales. Actually the captain didn't believe that I knew how to crew a sail vessel. I had gained my experience from several yachts in the New York harbor. Due to the fact that we were short on time, we only sailed along the beautiful coastline for two and a-half-hours.

The islands are beautiful by nature and sailing on the high seas is always the most peaceful experience for me. It was the perfect ending to a perfect trip.

U.S. Virgin Islands

Ritz Carlton Hotel, St. Thomas

Feeding a donkey

Le Madri Village, St. John

Ruins of a Sugar Mill, St. Croix

View of the sea, St. Thomas

Chapter 14
U.S. Virgin Islands: St. John, St. Thomas, and St. Croix

The U.S. Virgin Islands of St. Thomas, St. John and St. Croix are located east of Puerto Rico. English is the national language and it's spoken with a sing-song rhythm and a very laid back attitude.

St. John

I boarded a ferry from St. Thomas to St. John's, the island of love. St. John is very laid back, over populated with flower children from the 1960's. They probably packed their bags, landed in this wonderful paradise and decided never to leave.

My host, Kathy McLaughlin, chauffeured me to Villa Mistral. The road was appropriately named Chocolate Lane. I could relate to that. The villa had a panoramic view of the sea, mountains, and other villas perched on the hillsides. All along the mountainside, I saw tiled roofs of tropical pink, light green, peach or turquoise. The island is surrounded by many cove shaped beaches.

There were five bedrooms in different wings in the villa, cathedral ceilings, a private pool, eat-in kitchen, family room, living room, several verandahs, game room, gym and a floral garden. The Romanesque arches on the deck had been designed with conch shells incorporated into the structure. Villas are ideal for families, privacy or honeymooners. This villa rents for $6,900.00 per week in high season. Renting a villa can be cost effective for a group of ten people with double occupancy. A family of four or more can share the amenities of a villa and its privacy.

During the evening, I opened the French-doors of my suite, gazed up at the full moon, then turned on the Panama fan to catch the tropical breeze and listen to the swells beating against the shore. The sound of the waves was intoxicating. Evenings were filled with syncopated, competing sounds of crickets and birds chirping. It was very peaceful and beautiful, as I slept in my four poster bed covered with a mosquito net.

Wesley Thomas, my driver, entertained by creating Caribbean style music by scraping a dried pea pod against the ridges of a bamboo. He allowed me to taste fresh cut sugar cane. Later, he introduced me to the calabash, a hard fruit that is not edible. The shell is cut and used as bowls or maracas or other instruments. The only way to get around the island is by car or safari bus. Centerline Road, the main road, circles the entire island. The island people honk their horns as they drive pass, just to say hello or greet you.

Dinner at "Dinner with Andre," was a treat. Andre is a Frenchman, with his own restaurant. He thoroughly enjoys his craft. The restaurant features French nouvelle cuisine-style, but the portions are very large. The capacity of the restaurant is forty-four. I dined on creamy French scalloped potatoes, grilled lamb chops, poached Anjou pear, crème caramel, lime, and mango sorbet. Champagne flowed throughout the night. Andre shares the restaurant with Chilly Billy's, another restaurant, which operates during the day. "Dinner with Andre," is only open for dinner. The restaurant has one side with open French doors, from where I could hear the bustling street noise.

Some of the sights that I saw on the island included overlooks, Annaberg Plantation Ruins and Coral Bay. Lunch at Shipwreck Landing included fresh fish and chips. I also ordered several Rum punches and a Bush Wacker to get the flavor of the land. A Bush Wacker consists of: vodka, run, kahlua, baileys, amaretta, and crème de cocoa with nutmeg on top.

Dinner at Asolare, hosted by Winston Bennett, was served with an exquisite presentation of local dishes such as: baked sea trout, fresh string beans, and rice, which was cooked in chicken broth. I ordered fresh fruit and sorbet for dessert.

I arrived early one morning at Trunk Bay, it's a cove beach, with lots of amenities including: a snack bar, running water for a shower, toilets, life guard, snorkel rentals and beach chairs. I wanted to experience snuba diving (a cross between scuba and snorkeling). Frank Cummings, the instructor, was very patient with me. He gave me a five-minute lesson on how to maneuver under water, which confused me on land. I'm not a strong swimmer, but I thought I'd try it, just for the heck of it. As he was instructing, he commented, "For you to be so successful, how could you be so stupid?" I simply couldn't get used to the big flippers and the mask, I felt like a klutz on he beach, nothing made sense, but the minute I entered the water, all of his instructions came to fruition. Suddenly, I was at twenty feet below the surface. I couldn't believe I was maneuvering so easily through the water while observing the rich coral formations as the tropical fish passed by and looked on. I felt as if I was in a giant fish tank. One fish stopped dead in his path and dared me to come close. I was exposed to a new world of underwater life.

After an hour or so, I departed the beach and decided to go shopping again. I bought toe rings as gifts at the Coconut Trading Co. for my television crew of "GlobeTrotter with Jon Haggins" and painted key holders made from oil drums. I also bought Blind Betty's hot sauce. There were several other sauces such as: Jolly Dog, Hot Caribbean Concoctions, and Pineapple Pizzazz. The boutique was filled with mugs, hats, and caps, T-shirts, greeting and post cards, clothing and CD's. Ellen, the sales clerk, was very informative about the island. She talked about how, after taking a vacation to the island, she decided to pack up and move there.

I met a family, and asked how were they spending their vacation. They informed me that they had joined another family and rented two yachts. Each family has five children, age ranging from seven to seventeen. They love the water and all the water sports such as: snorkeling, scuba, water skiing and just plain old swimming. They also use the boat to bond. Everyone has chores, whether dinghy captain, mooring the boat, or doing dishes. They were there during a school semester, so they saved time each day for doing homework. One of the mothers shared a little inside info:

the two families play games with one another and cook together in the galley.

St. John, is truly an island for lovers—it's the island of love.

St. Thomas

After an afternoon of browsing and lunch, I boarded a ferryboat, destined for St. Thomas.

Joey Bradshaw, the driver, met me at the dock and transported me in a Safari Bus to the Ritz Carlton Hotel. The Ritz is everything you'd expect. It's a luscious palatial property with spacious suites facing the manicured gardens and the sea, designer swimming pool, beach, health club and a children's recreation room. A variety of entertainment is provided each night of the week.

After a brisk check-in, I was off to dinner in the main dining room. The dining room is rather formal. Men are required to wear shirts with long sleeves or a jacket. It doesn't matter what you eat on the island, 'cause everything is delicious and carefully prepared.

The next morning, I ventured off to have breakfast at the Marriott Frenchman's Reef with host Nick Pourzsal, the General Manager. There was one table of just fresh fruit. There were also the usual – eggs, bacon, pancakes etc.

There is nightly entertainment at the Wine Bar with different entertainment each night. The Gym has a trainer. I also toured the suites; they were well appointed, overlooking the cove and sea. They also have meeting and changing rooms next to the pool. I especially loved the wedding gazebo, just because I love gazebos.

Later that afternoon, I went sailing. No vacation is a vacation without a cruise on a yacht. Ian Hughes, was the captain of this yacht, he looked like a young Lloyd Bridges. He originally lived in Toronto, Canada, and then decided to take his vessel into the high seas. It took him two months to sail from Canada on his forty-four foot vessel to St. Thomas. Ian's yacht can be chartered for six or a maximum of eight guests, plus a crew of two. Seven-night charters cost $4,450 plus tax $135 (all-inclusive: food and alcohol) during the low season and $5,900 plus tax for the high season. The advantage of chartering a boat is that you can go from port to port through the crystal blue and aqua marine waters. He also leases out the vessel for day trips. The boat is also available without a crew (bare boat). But you have to have a captain's license and prove that you can handle the boat.

On the island of St. Thomas is Coral World Marine Park and Underwater Observatory. It has a wonderful collection of tropical fish in an oversized circular tank. The tank allows the fish to swim with the flow. Posters along the wall identify all the fish. The grand tour included a stairwell that led down to the basin of the sea. From that room, one can see the fish in their natural habitat. You are actually peering into their world at the bottom of the sea. It is a real live aquarium.

Later that evening, I dined at, "Dinner at Herve." I didn't meet a dish I didn't like. After dinner someone suggested ordering different deserts and passing them around the table to sample. Well, at the end of dinner, someone got stuck with twelve deserts.

Next day, I ventured to yet another shopping mall, Royal Davie's Mall, on Main Street. The street is lined with assorted shops such as: jewelry stores, liquor, clothing at discount prices and more. I stopped for lunch at Glady's Café. I had heard so much about her cuisine and wanted to try it for myself. I sat and immediately ordered a rum punch, flavored with bananas and spice drink. Glady's served typical island cuisine; conch in lemon butter sauce, conch fritters, fungi and plantains or Gladys' hot chicken salad. She also makes gazpacho and conch chowder.

One of the last experiences on the island of St. Thomas was taking the Gondola Tram ride up the mountainside. The cost of the ride is $6.00 each way. It was a clear day and the harbor was filled with cruise ships. St. Thomas is a major destination for cruise ships. The journey up the mountain was exhilarating because I felt suspended as the tram proceeded to a height of 700 feet. When I reached the top, I discovered lots of shops and an open bar with tropical drinks and a view of the harbor.

St. Croix

When I arrived at the dock in St. Thomas a baggage man asked if I was going to my yacht. "Yacht?" I remarked. "No I'm taking the seaplane. Up, up and away as we propelled to St. Croix. The cost of the plane is $55.00 per person one way. From my window I saw many lush green islands. St. Croix, the largest of the three main islands, is flatter. We landed at Kings Landing Yacht Club in Christiansted, St. Croix, the port is located in the heart of the town, just across the road from Fort Christiansted. During war times, the fort was used to protect the island and fight off the enemies.

Sweeney Troussaint, the driver, met me. He was knowledgeable regarding the island because he had been president of the Hotel Association for three years. Now, he enjoys showing off his island to tourists. Sweeney drove along the winding narrow roads to the Buccaneer Resort. At the entrance gate, there was a sign that read, "Please inform the guard of the nature of your visit." I immediately interpreted it as, "State Your Business." Elizabeth Armstrong, the hotel's owner, greeted me as I arrived. After another speedy check in, I freshened up for dinner in the hotel's dining room. I had been looking for escargot prepared in butter and garlic sauce from the moment I arrived. This was the best!

The Buccaneer property has one of the best 18-hole golf courses (cost $25.00 per game during the off season and $50.00 during high season), nine tennis courts, two restaurants, private villas with spacious suites, a children's program, two pools and a picturesque stretch of beach. The grounds are filled with tropical flowers, such as: golden trumpet flower, orchids, bougainvillea etc. The suites with ocean views are $235 low season and $335 high season. They even have a widows' suite. It got its name from the widows, who waited for their seamen to return. The floors are laid with Italian marble.

In 1756, the Danish purchased the island of St. Croix. Africans were brought to the island to work on the sugar cane plantations. St. Croix no longer produces sugar cane, but does import molasses. St. Croix produces eight different blends of Rum. Peter Van Stoten, a Danish governor, freed the slaves in 1849 in Frederiksted (another fort on the other side of town) after an up rising. Slaves had been promised they would be set free. Those promises never came to fruition, so they took it into their hands and threatened to burn the town if they were not set free. He finally granted their wish and was put into prison by the King. However, his order was not revoked and the slaves remained free.

In 1917, the United States purchased the Virgin Islands for twenty five million dollars. Ten years after the sale, the people of the U.S. Virgin Island were granted citizenship. People have migrated to St. Croix from Canada, Middle East, the United States and Europe. St. Croix has a population of about 50,000. Today, there are 4,000 people who have moved there from the United States. The island has lots of historic, non-working windmills as monuments to their history.

On Harbor Night (when cruise ships arrive), they light up the squares and fill them with jammin' steel drums, reggae music, assorted foods and souvenir vendors. It's a great celebration, because vendors have an opportunity to sell their wares.

Next morning, I visited the Botanical Gardens, an expansive national park with a variety of plants and trees. There were Royal Palm trees and remains of crammed slave quarters. Forty slaves slept in a twenty-four by twelve room. I also visited the Whim Plantation. The plantation dates back to 1774. It's a Neo-Classic structure that sits on 150 acres of sugar plantation. The house is built with no steel, just stone, sand, molasses, and seashells to cement the stones.

Sylvia Emomen, the tour guide, escorted us from room to room in the main building. She enlightened us with the history of the house and its décor. There was a catalog where one could order reproductions of the furniture that decorated the house. Her good manner and attitude reminded me of the southern ladies from the states. The home was built with mahogany floors with just three rooms, living room, dining room and bedroom. The kitchen was located in another building in back of the main house. As I passed through the door, a young lady offered me one of the donuts she had just baked.

I think the most unusual experience in St. Croix, was to visit the beer-drinking hogs in a coral outside of the city. Guests were requested to purchase cans of beer at the store next door, then hand it to the hogs. The hogs reached and crushed the can with their mouths and devoured the beer. Have you heard the expression, "You eat like a pig?" Well, they drank like hogs.

Later, after we drove back to town, I took a brisk walk along Kings' Alley and had lunch at Wa-Hoo Willie Restaurant. The bartender made a concoction called the Willie Wacker. It consists of mango, pineapple rum, coconut rum and crème of coconut. The national Rum is Cruzan and it's very inexpensive to purchase. Cruzan is a slave language. Slaves used to disguise their messages with a song. They would sing (Cariso) and smile at the plantation owner while mimicking them.

One evening, I took a hike up to the Rattan Inn (a small bed and breakfast). It's decorated with rattan and Oriental Chippendale furniture. The inn is located on a hilltop with a wrought iron entrance gate. Infee Hong-Covell, the owner (Korean), prepared fresh sushi as a treat for my visit.

My final day was spent on a Catamaran cruise. Captain Big Beard and Captain Simpson manned the vessel, which can hold thirty-seven passengers. We sailed from the harbor, with the main sail up. The wind was brisk; it was a perfect day to sail to Buck Island, an uninhabited national park and game reserve where we could also snorkel and picnic.

I met several couples on the boat who were spending their honeymoon on the island. The cost for the day cruise is $65.00 including lunch and snorkel equipment. The cruise also includes a snorkel guide. I dipped into the water and was maneuvering very well until a few waves rushed me and filled my mask. Suddenly, I panicked, removed the mask and swam to the ring for support. Once I caught my breath and relaxed, I turned and headed back to the boat. Lunch was a combination of hot dogs, fish and hamburgers. The captain prepared lunch over a barbecue pit on Buck Island's beach. Rum punch, soda, beer or water chased it down.

I received a gift of a sterling silver hook love bracelet from The Caribbean Bracelet Company. The shop has an extensive collection of gold and silver bracelets for every taste. There is no island tax on purchases. All goods are sold at the same price as the duty free shops. As I browsed through this quaint little shop, I imagined buying all those especially designed items for friends back home.

It was not easy to have to depart this lush land with friendly people and warm balmy winds from the sea.

Jamaica

Coral Reef Inn, Negril

Lighthouse in Negril, Jamaica

Jamaica Inn in Ocho Rios

Colonial buildings, Jamaica

Bob Marley mural in Ocho Rios

Chapter 15
Jamaica—Family Run Inns

Jamaica is the home of Bob Marley. There are lots of beaches and a laid back attitude. It's the innermost Caribbean Island with lots of personality. The island is known for its jerk sauce and reggae music.

After a three and a half-hour flight from JFK on American Airlines, I arrived at Donald Sangster International Airport in Montego Bay, Jamaica. I was pleasantly surprised that the Black Jamaicans' posture, poise and manners reminded me of West Africans. The temperature was extremely hot. I began peeling off my clothes the minute I exited the plane. The Jamaicans were casual and relaxed, a place I wanted my head to be. They greeted me with a gentle hospitable smile. "Ya-Mon" and "Irie" was heard all over the island. "Irie" means, "Yes I agree with you" and "That's cooool to whatever you say".

After I cleared customs, Paula Dykes, from the Jamaican Tourist Board and driver, Barrington Edwards, greeted me. Barrington was sitting in the driver's seat on the right side of the car. At first I thought he was a passenger. It was not easy for me to visualize driving on the left side of the road. Paula & Barry shared their humor and created a very relaxed atmosphere. "No problem, Mon", was also often heard.

During the drive along the coast to Ocho Rios, there was the Caribbean Sea following us on the left. The vivid tropical color waters of turquoise, aqua with grand white swells rushed to the shore. Overhead was a clear blue sky. I visualized this as an impressionist painting in my mind. We stopped at a roadside cafe and purchased a basket of jerk chicken and pork. I splashed on a little jerk sauce to spice it up. Well, my mouth was on fire; it began to sizzle. Immediately, I ordered a very cold Red Stripe beer to soothe the sensation.

After lunch, we trailed the long, narrow, winding, sometimes one-lane roads around and through the mountains. Men walked along the roadside swinging their arms with a rhythm (a la Jamaican). There were many sleeping policemen in the cities. A sleeping policeman is a bump in the road to reduce the speed of traffic.

After a two-hour drive, we checked in at the Village Inn. A lovely family of three owns the property – Mr. Stephenson, his wife and daughter. They run a very efficient inn right in the heart of Ocho Rios. It's located within a short walking distance from everything that's shoppable or edible. Mr. Stephenson hosted a family style dinner with his daughter. I call it family style because everyone sat around a very large table and passed the dishes around. Dinner was an assorted collection of Jamaican cuisine such as: conch soup, jerk chicken, rice covered with onions and spices, seafood salad, a green salad and coconut deserts.

The Little Pub was just a skip away from the Inn. On stage was a jammin' energetic trio playing Reggae/Socca music. The keyboard player was the highlight of the band with his acrobatic movements. The vocalist sounded like a black Tom Jones, but looked like Barry White. On another night the jammin' was held at an open outdoor space with blaring reggae and hip-hop music. One of the local characters wore a loose fitting outfit that looked like pajamas. He gyrated his slim body while flinging his arms in every direction at once. I called it, "The pajama dance."

The next morning, we drove over to Dunn's River Falls, in Ocho Rios, it's an adventure not to be missed. The fall reaches 600 feet into the sky, built of limestone rocks with a continuous spring flowing down into the sea. I climbed halfway up holding hands, feet or whatever to survive the climb. Then I began climbing with all fours, I was petrified, frozen against the rocks as the water flowed over my body into the sea. Midstream, I looked down, which is what I was told not to do, then looked up and froze for a few minutes. I was afraid I would slip and end it all. I knew I couldn't go down or up. "What am I going to do?" I asked myself. I had no choice but to continue until I saw an exit, then walked back to the beach where I boarded a local fishing boat to motor to the Hibiscus Inn for lunch. There were large catamarans and sailing yachts cruising casually along as we motored to the dock. I felt like I was on a dingy by comparison.

From the boat, we climbed a wall of steep stairs to the Hibiscus Inn's restaurant overlooking the sea. Lunch was buffet style with assorted Jamaican dishes. My favorite was the potent rum balls for desert. But there were also plantains, tarts, etc. The bungalows at the inn shared a pool overlooking the sea.

Along the coast is the Jamaican Inn, which sits on seven pristine manicured acres with a pool overlooking the sea. The spacious suites have oversized verandahs where one can gaze at the sea or just relax. There was an abundance of small yellow butterflies playfully scattering about from palm tree to palm tree. The white suite, with wooden shutters that open onto the sea is usually reserved a year in advance for honeymooners or newlyweds. It's romantically perched directly over the sea with an uninterrupted view of the tropical world. Jamaica is a perfect place to share a honeymoon or wedding. Many properties arrange the entire occasion to your specifications at a fraction of the cost of a wedding in the States. The Inn is very English in style and expensively formal.

The manager of the inn informed me that fishing is outlawed from June 'til August. This allows the fish to spawn. One day he discovered a man on the beach who had caught a large turtle. He offered to sell it to the manager. The manager informed him that it was against the law to fish in July. The man responded, "I'm not fishing, "Can't ya see, mon? This is a turtle." "Fish, turtle, what's the difference?" replied the manager. The manager purchased the turtle and released it into the sea. The turtle ran into the waters at the speed of light, never to return to pay his debt.

After a comfy afternoon at the inn, I decided I wanted a little more adventure so I ventured out to White River for tube rafting. It's probably one of the most exciting experiences in Ocho Rios. The entrance is at the mouth at the top of the mountain. I peeled down to my red swim trunks and entered the cool water with a wooden paddle in hand.

A cord attached the tube to a wooden bottom. Initially I was disoriented; I couldn't get my groove. I began spinning in circles while the rest of the tourists left me far behind. Finally, I caught up with everyone with the help of the rapids, then bumped against the shore. Suddenly, I was grounded. I lost my balance, fell out of the tube and was pulled by the force of the stream. I tried to lift myself into the tube but got whacked on the head by the wooden bottom as everyone laughed. When I composed myself and got back in, I continued smoothly under the thick green forest of an array of swaying bamboo trees. As I laid on my back and continued down the rapids, I observed the sun trying to peek through the trees.

Next morning, I visited Coyaba River Gardens, as I entered the gates, I realized we had climbed 500 feet into the hills to an oasis in the heavens. There were birds chirping and rustling leaves in a beautifully designed tropical floral and vegetation sanctuary, with wooden plank bridges over a free flowing, fresh spring waterfall. The spring supplies the entire city of Ocho Rios with water. The estate houses a museum of artifacts depicting the history of Jamaica. This was the essence of Jamaica.

Every road leads to a shopping market. Shopping is big time fun in Jamaica. The American dollar goes a long way, $35.00 JA equals $1.00 US. There are tourist craft markets everywhere with woodcarvings, fabrics, beads, paintings, baskets and other assorted gifts for friends back home. There are also large open produce markets of assorted colorful offerings of ackee (looks like eggs), salted codfish, fresh papayas, fruits, callalou greens, bananas, bread fruit (taste like potatoes when boiled) and cassava (good for the nerves).

I met some Americans and while walking with them, I asked, "Mon, ya want a taxi"? A Jamaican man yelled, "Ya trying make fun of me, Ya-Mon," I replied, "I don't even know you." Then he called me a coconut. I responded, "Thank you," and continued to walk. When I returned to the hotel, I asked the receptionist what does "a coconut" mean. She was reluctant to tell me, but I coaxed her. She informed me, "It means, white on the inside and black on the outside". I told her that he couldn't have been talking about me.

After all this walking and talking, I had to satisfy my appetite. One of the most decorative dinners was designed by the cook/owner of Tradewinds. There were seven courses. Everything was so continental, beautiful and fresh. Even the plates were decorative. The owner told us that for her creative expression, she designs different dishes everyday. In the middle of the seven courses, we were served a sorbet to cleanse the palate.

Next morning I departed Ocho Rios, en route to Montego Bay. I resided at Doctor Cave's Beach Hotel. Andre McGann is the owner and manager. The hotel is located on "Hip Strip," the main drag, the pulse of the town. It's just a short walk from Margaritaville. Margaritaville is a lively youthful joint suspended over the sea with a waterslide from the second floor. Once you enter the slide, the flowing water propels you down into the sea. Margaritaville serves delicious fruit flavored drinks including margaritas. They are like thick sorbet with frozen tropical flavors. The young crowd that gathers late in the evening creates the lively atmosphere. There is a cabaret upstairs and a disco downstairs.

Jamaica's Tourist Office offers a "Meet the people program." We were invited to the home of Beverly Russell and her daughter. Their home was a sprawling estate located on a private beachfront property with an open-air family room onto the verandah. We shared dinner with the hosts and other guests from the Jamaican Tourist Board. The evening's home cooked meal was another addition to the pleasure of visiting Jamaica. Dinner included chicken stuffed with ackee, pork with its skin, rice and vegetables and lots of assorted deserts.

We were driven over to the Relax Resort, which is located on the side of a mountain overlooking the city we were served curried chicken, rice and vegetables and ice cream for desert. The landscape upon our return to Doctor's Cave Inn varied from luscious villas to cow pastures to tourist spots.

P.J.'s is an outdoor Jamaican cabaret with a live reggae band. The fire eating eighty-year-old man mesmerized me. He twisted and contorted his lean, wiry body into all kinds of yoga positions. Off stage, he could barely walk, but on stage, he danced to the pulse of the jammin' music. Nightlife doesn't start there until after midnight.

I cruised on the semi, sub glass bottom boat. It appeared to have submerged twenty-five feet through the magnifying glass. One of the crew swam around the boat attracting a frenzied collection of tropical fish. He even swam with a smile while blowing circular rings of air from his mouth. Several tourists jumped into the sea to snorkel while I watched.

History and legend play vital roles in what to see and do. In the heart of Mobay is Sam Sharpe's Square. It's named after one of Jamaica's emancipation patriots who led the Rebellion of 1831. Sharpe served as deacon at historic Burchell Memorial Church built in 1824. The slave leader was captured and hanged in Mobay. Mr. Sharpe has become a national hero. Nearby, the square also holds the Ring, where captives were traded and caged. They incarcerated runaway captives, disorderly seamen and other vagrants.

Legends abound of wicked Annie Palmer, the white witch of Rose Hall. Rose Hall is located on the hillside in Mobay, overlooking the ocean. It is believed she killed three husbands, and then was killed by her slave lover. My tour of this haunted house, conjured up images of ghosts dancing and running throughout the house, spreading maccumba spirits that never rest.

To top off this tour, I visited Negril. A very laid back resort with not much to do except lay back and enjoy. The Marina's Inn has a number of two story bungalows facing the sea. I was surprised there were no phones or televisions in the suites. A family of seven brothers owns the Inn. Carey Wallace is the oldest. He played the fender bass with a reggae band. The lively reggae quartet and energetic vocalist performed during dinner. Negril is my kind of town. Mike Regan, a writer from Philadelphia, who I met on the trip, was a gutsy sorta guy. He had a sense of adventure. He'd try anything. He dived twice off the lighthouse tower into the sea, so I could photograph him. He played bass with the band. He also jumped in the sea off the semi sub to snorkel. On the beach, he played soccer against two Brazilians. And guess who won? I called him Mickey, because he ate everything that wasn't nailed down.

I was impressed with the small family run inns that I visited because all but one was owned and operated by black families. The families always made me feel welcome as if I were visiting their home.

Jackies' on the Reef in Negril is a terrific place if you're into meditation or holistic healing. The main building is located on the reef with the Caribbean Sea beating against the shore. There is a very large oval shape verandah on which to relax. On the ground there are several private cottages with open-air suites and bath. There is a community kitchen with all the healthy goodies your heart desires. I say, if you're bad and want to be beaten with a palm leaf, this is the place. Many people come for a minimum of four days to relieve themselves of stress. I saw several women receiving massages stretched out on tables under the sun overlooking the sea. If I have to say one thing, "It's peaceful."

My favorite inn in Negril, was the Coral Sea Resort, it's located on a seven-mile stretch of white sand beach. Once you step through the French doors, you're one step closer to the restaurant and bar and a fingernail from the beach. Each bungalow is named after the scented flower that's planted at its doorstep. The suites are spaciously open and appealing for honeymooners or just ordinary folk like me.

Imagine a turquoise sea and the chalk white beach sans people. It was soothing and tranquil. I walked on sand barges for miles into the sea; the water level remained at my knees. I think for the first time in my life, I swam and floated on my back, looking up at the beautiful blue clear tropical sky, for an hour without resting. It was the most relaxing thing I've ever done.

Grenada

Food market in St. George's Open Market

Queen's Harbor

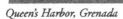

Queen's Harbor, Grenada

Water fall, Grenada

Boat builder's children

Chapter 16
Grenada, A Spice To Savor

Grenada is known as a spice island, located in the Caribbean, just north of the island of Trinidad.

I was flown on the most entertaining American Airlines flight. One of the flight attendants amused the passengers with a bit of humor: "Smoking is not permitted on this flight. However, if you insist on smoking, please step out on the wing." She had a captive audience and the entire plane roared with laughter.

Grenada is known for its spices and I could almost smell the aromas as the plane landed at Point Salines Airport. From the moment I stepped out of the plane, I knew I was going to enjoy the land of the spices. Edwin Frank and Liz Gorman, from the Grenada Tourist Office, greeted me with a rum punch welcome drink. The island also features fresh fruit punch such as papaya, guava etc. The temperature was Hot! Hot! Hot! Just the way I like it.

Frank (another Frank), the driver, was an amicable young man, always with a smile. Everyone drives on the left side of the road. My home base was at the Rex Grenadian Resorts Hotel, a lush property that sits on 38 acres directly on the beach. The hotel is only five minutes from the airport. Surprisingly, I didn't hear any noise from the airport. The low season single room rate starts at approximately $165.00 US without meals.

Grenada is celebrating its twenty-fifth anniversary of independence from Great Britain. It has a population of ninety-six thousand, made up of Africans, East Indians and people of European descent. The currency is 2.67 E.C. (Eastern Caribbean) = $1.00 U.S. English is the national language. Grenada is a tri-island nation, which consist of Carriacou and Petite Martinique. Parishes divide the island, instead of towns or neighborhoods. Creeks and rivers separate the parishes.

The island is twenty-one miles long with open, lush greens, volcanic beaches, and friendly trade winds, swaying forests, tropical rains and unpolluted waters. The sound of the water fills the air. Grenada receives approximately 400 cruise ships per year. There are chartered yachts available for the length of your stay. The Arawak Indians settled on the island before Columbus.

There are many narrow, winding roads. Several traffic lights have been installed recently. Three, traffic signal directing policemen have been permanently positioned as a tourist attraction. The policemen have a grand stylistic motion that they perform with their hands as they wave the traffic through. The officers were very graceful and poised; their hands moved as if they were performing a ballet. Tourism is the number one industry for the island. I was told that one could be jailed for cursing an officer of the law or for drugs.

Grenada is the land of spices such as nutmeg, cocoa for expensive chocolates and bananas. I salivated over the nutmeg ice cream after dinner. St. George's open air market has fresh picked fruits, vegetables, lots of callaloo and spices such as: allspice blended with rum for black cake (wedding cake), tunka and vanilla beans. Some of the island's favorite dishes are jerk chicken, flying fish in a sauce, breadfruit, cocoa bread (spoon bread), callaloo, rice and peas, stewed beef, and oxtails etc

Carriacou Island is just two a two hour Osprey Express ferry ride across the Caribbean Sea. And Petite Martinique is a small island just off the coast. It's known as the land of reefs. As the ferry sped off from Queen's Harbor into the sea, I observed a collection of locals standing at the front of the boat on the top deck, while I viewed the shoreline. Suddenly, they kneeled behind a partition and I was splashed by a wave. I was soaked from head to toe. I felt like a wet duck, but I was still laughing. Each time the locals ducked, I was hit by another big splash. There was nothing I could do about it, but lay and get sun dried before exiting onto the island of Petite Martinique.

Every January, Grenada has a sailing tournament from Union Island to Queen's Harbor. I took a ferry to Petite Martinique. The island is known as a boat-building colony. The entire island participates in a huge celebration of the launching of each wooden vessel. I talked with Clayton De Rouche, a famous local boat builder of sailing and fishing vessels. He builds only three or four boats each year and stamps them with his dragon logo.

All boats are registered at the Port in Grenada. Ninety-nine point nine percent of the island is Catholic. Petite Martinique is a small island that is family oriented. I asked my hostess if everyone on the island was related. She asked why I wondered that. "Everyone has honey color skin and similar facial features," I answered. Many were her cousins. Their families consist of numerous offspring. Maybe it's because men drink goat water. Goat water is similar to Viagra. Petite Martinique is a very tranquil island surrounded by turquoise water.

We boarded a fisherman's boat for a short trip to the Island of Carriacou. We passed a solo island that was filled with piles of white conch shells. I lunched at the Silver Beach Cottages, which has fourteen rooms located on the beach. There are lots of holiday cottages on the West Coast and three hotels. No one is allowed to build higher than the tallest palm tree. After lunch, I relaxed on Paradise beach and walked along the shoreline to collect conch shells, which were plentiful along the fine white beach sand. Later that afternoon, I laid on my back and floated in the salted sea to gaze out into the turquoise waters. Camute Caliste is the most famous artist in Carriacou and several of his murals are spread around the island. Throughout my drive around the island I noticed oysters rooted at the bottom of the mangrove trees. Carriacou is a very quiet resort, for a day trip or overnight at most.

Another great treasure of Grenada is Sandy Island. Sandy Island, viewed from the ferry, describes itself as a dream oasis with tall swaying palm tress and a beautiful white sand beach. Many vessels moor along the coast to enjoy the fresh unspoiled environment of the island and the sheer pleasure of it all.

Queens Park Road is on the big island of Grenada. While driving along the road I saw several breathtaking waterfalls. The West Coast is lined with small villages. Morne Fendue Plantation house was built in 1908 on

16 acres high into the hills. I lunched there and felt taken back in time. There are carvings of indigenous people in the rocks. The house sits on top of a mountain and provides guests with a glimpse of the Spice Isle's heritage. Authentic Island Plantation was built out of colorful stones from nearby rivers. They were hauled by oxen and chiseled to fit.

A short distance away is the Grand Etang National Park, where I photographed a Mona monkey as he approached me. This mountainous island is formed from volcanic rock, which today, is covered with bougainvillea and a variety of hibiscus and orchids. There are also lush green palm trees and vegetation everywhere.

One of Grenada tourist attractions is Leapers' Hill, where Blacks would not submit to French Sauteurs as slaves, but instead leaped to their death.

La Source Resorts is one of the most exclusive all-inclusive hotel properties on the island. All amenities, including massages, are included. The hotel is located on thirty-eight acres next to the beach. My dinner was a la carte which is what I prefer. I hate buffets because the display confuses and fills me up.

For an American dollar, I received a guided tour of Fort Frederick where Grenada gained its independence. The highest point on the island is Mount St. Catherine at 2,756 feet above sea level. Fort George was names after King George 111. There are three forts; one is used as a prison. Local prisoners construct furniture and grow vegetables that can be purchased. In 1983, the Fort Matthew's Barracks, now a museum and a police headquarters, was the location where Prime Minister Maurice Bishop was shot during a coup. I saw the bullet holes in the pole where they lined him up.

At Sur La Mer Restaurant, Mama Miriam, the proprietor, was the entertainment. She was animated and sang instead of talked. Her conversation was always in a song. Her property is located directly on the beach. I walked out and laid on a chaise between lunch courses. There was so much food, I was afraid I'd gain too much weight for my swimming trunks.

My last night was spent at the Flamboyant Hotel on the beach. It has sixty rooms and is still growing. There was a crab race after a delightful dinner of assorted dishes. I actually bet on a crab and won.

I returned home with the aroma of the spices around my neck. Grenada is a spice to remember.

Appendix A
Embassies and Consulates

You can obtain a tourist travel visa at:

Benin

Entry regulations: Passport: Visa

Embassy of Benin
2737 Cathedral Ave. NW
Washington, DC 20008
202-232-6656/ fax: 202-235-1996

Permanent Mission of Benin
4 East 73rd St.
New York City, NY 10021
212-249-6014/fax: 212-734-4735

Brazil

Diplomatic Information: Entry regulations: Passport: Visa

Brazilian Embassy
3006 Massachusetts Ave. NW
Washington, DC 20008
202-745-2828/fax: 202-745-2827

Brazilian Consulate General
Boston, MA
617-542-4000/fax: 617-542-4318

Chicago, IL
312-464-0244/fax: 312-464-0299

Los Angeles, CA
213-651-2664/fax: 213-651-2664

Miami, FL
305-285-6200/fax: 305-285-6229

New York, NY
212-757-3080/fax: 212-956-3794

San Francisco, CA
415-981-8170/fax: 415-981-3628

Houston, TX
713-961-3063/fax: 713-961-3070

Burkina Faso

Diplomatic Information: Entry regulations: Passport, Visa

Embassy of Burkina Faso
2340 Massachusetts Ave. NW
Washington, DC 20008
202-332-5577/fax: 202-667-1882

Cote D'Ivoire

Diplomatic information Entry regulations: Passport; Visa for stay over 90
days

Embassy of Cote D'Ivoire
2424 Massachusetts Ave. NW
Washington, DC 20008
202-797-0300/fax: 202-462-9444

Cote D'Ivoire Honorary Consulate
645 Griswold, Suite 244

Detroit, MI 48226
313-961-9000/fax: 313-964-3233

Tourist information:

Cote D'Ivoire Tourist Office
2412 Massachusetts Ave. NW
Washington, DC 20008
202-797-0344/fax: 202-387-6381

Ecuador

Entry Regulations: Passport; Visa for stay over 90 days; onward ticket.

Embassy of Ecuador
15th St. NW
Washington, DC 20009
202-234-7200/fax: 202-265-6385

Consulate General of Ecuador
Beverly Hills, CA
323-658-6020/fax: 323-658-1934

Chicago, IL
312-329-0266/fax: 312-329-0359

Houston, TX
713-622-1787/fax: 713-622-1787

Jersey City, NJ
201-985-1300/fax: 201-985-2959

New York City, NY
212-808-0171/fax: 212-808-0188

Tourist Information

Ministerio de Turismo
Ave Eloy Alfaro 1214
Quito, Ecuador
5932-224-970/fax: 5932-229-330
Rocio Vasquez, Minister

Egypt

Diplomatic information

Entry regulations: Passport, Visa

Embassy of the Arab Republic of Egypt
3521 International Court NW
Washington, DC 20008
202-895-5400/fax: 202-828-9167

Consulate General of Egypt:

Chicago, IL
312-828-9162/fax: 312-828-9167

Houston, TX
713-961-4915/fax: 713-961-3868

New York, NY
212-759-7120/fax: 212-308-7643

San Francisco, CA
415-346-9700/fax: 415-346-9480

Tourist information:

Egyptian Tourist Authority
83-83 Wilshire Blvd., Suite 215
Los Angeles, CA 90211
213-653-8815/fax: 213-653-8961

Egyptian Tourist Authority
630 Fifth Ave., Suite 1706
New York City, NY 10111
212-332-2570/fax: 212-956-6439

Egyptian Consulate General
1110 Second Ave.
New York City 10022
212-759-7120

Fiji

Diplomatic Information

Entry Regulations: Passport; sufficient funds; onward ticket; Visa for 1-month stay issued on arrival.

Fiji Embassy
2233 Wisconsin Avenue NW, Suite 240
Washington, DC 20007
202-337-8320/fax: 202-337-1996

Tourist Information

Fiji Visitors Bureau
Thomson St, GPO Box 92
Suva, Fiji
679-302-433/fax: 679-300-970
Sitiveni Yagona, CEO

Fiji Visitors Bureau
5777 W. Century Blvd, Suite 220
Los Angeles, CA 90045
800-932-3454
310-568-1616/fax: 310-670-2318
Joe Tuamoto, Reg. Director Americas

Gambia

Diplomatic information: Entry regulations: Passport, Visa

Gambia Embassy
1155 15th St., NW, Suite 1000
Washington, DC 20005
202-785-1399/fax: 202-785-1430

Permanent Mission of Gambia
820 Second Ave., Suite 900C
New York City 10017
212-949-6640/fax: 212-856-9820

Ghana

Diplomatic information

Entry regulations; Passport, Visa, yellow fever shot, for stays over 7 days visitors must register at Ghana Immigration Service within 48 hours.

Embassy of Ghana
3512 International Dr. NW
Washington, DC 20008
202-686-4500/fax: 202-686-4527

Consulate General of Ghana
19 East 47th St.
New York City 10017
212-832-1300/fax: 212-751-6743

Kenya

Diplomatic information

Entry regulations: Passport, Visa

Embassy of Kenya
2249 "R" St. NW
Washington, DC 20008
202-387-6101/fax: 202-462-3829

Mali

Diplomatic information

Entry regulations: Passport; Visa

Embassy of the Republic of Mali
2130 "R" St. NW
Washington, DC 20008
202-332-2249/fax: 202-332-6603

Permanent Mission of Mali
111 East 69th St.
New York City 10021
212-737-4150/fax: 212-472-3778

Morocco

Diplomatic information

Entry regulations: Passport; Visa for stay over 3 months

Embassy of Morocco
1601 21st St. NW
Washington, DC 20009
202-462-7979/fax: 202-265-0161

Consulate General of Morocco
10 East 40th Street
New York City, NY 10016
212-213-9644/fax: 212-779-7441

Tourist information:

Moroccan National Tourist Office
20 East 46th St.
New York City 10017
212-557-2520/fax: 212-949-8148

Senegal

Diplomatic information

Entry regulations: Passport: onward ticket; yellow fever vaccination: Visa for stay over 3 months.

Senegal Embassy
2112 Wyoming Ave. NW
Washington, DC 20008
202-234-0540/fax: 202-332-6315

Senegal Tourist Office
350 Fifth Avenue
New York City, NY 10001
212-279-1953/fax: 212-279-1958

South Africa:

Diplomatic information

Entry regulations: Passport; Visa

The South African Embassy
3051 Massachusetts Ave. NW
Washington, DC 20008
202-232-4400/fax: 202-265-1607

The South African Consulate General:

Beverly Hills, CA
310-657-9200/fax: 310- 657-9215

Chicago, IL
312-939-7929/fax: 312-939-7481

New York, NY
212-213-4880/fax: 212-213-0102

Tourist information:

South African Tourism Board
800-822-5368
New York, NY
212-730-2929/fax: 212-764-1980

Los Angeles, CA
310-641-8444/fax: 310-641-5812

Tanzania

Diplomatic information

Entry regulations: Passport; Visa

Embassy of Tanzania
2139 "R" St. NW
Washington, DC 20008
202-939-6125/fax: 202-797-7408

Permanent Mission of Tanzania
205 East 42nd St., Room 1300

New York City, NY 10017
212-972-9160/fax: 212-682-5232

Uruguay

Diplomatic Information

Entry Regulations: Passport; Visa for stay over 3 months

Embassy of Uruguay
2715 M St. NW, 3rd floor
Washington, DC 20007
202-331-1313/fax: 202-331-8142

Consulate General of Uruguay

Coral Gables, FL
305-443-9764/fax: 305-443-7802

New York City, NY
212-753-8191/fax: 212-753-8591

Santa Monica, CA
210-394-5777/fax: 310-394-5140

Tourist Information

Ministry of Tourism
Ave Del Libertador 1409
Montevideo, CP-1110 Uruguay
5982-989-105/fax: 5982-921-624

Uruguayan Tourism Office
1077 Ponce de Leon Blvd.
Coral Gables, FL 33134
305-443-7431/fax: 305-443-7431

Zimbabwe

Diplomatic information

Entry regulations: Passport, onward ticket

Embassy of Zimbabwe
1608 New Hampshire Ave. NW

Washington, DC 20009
202-332-7100/fax: 202-483-9326

Permanent Mission of Zimbabwe
128 East 56th St.
New York City, NY 10022
212-980-9511/fax: 212-755-4188

Tourist information:

Zimbabwe Tourist Office
1270 Ave. of the Americas, Suite 412
New York City 10020
800-621-2381
212-332-1090/fax: 212-332-1093

For entry to many of the Caribbean Islands you need proof of citizenship; photo ID, an onward ticket, and sufficient funds.

Reference to Travel Agent Official Travel Industry Directory.

Appendix B
Departments of Tourism

U.S. Virgin Islands Dept. of Tourism
PO Box 6400
St. Thomas, U.S.V.I. 00804
Phone -340-774-8784
Fax -340-774-4390

Grenada Board of Tourism-USA
820 Second Avenue, Suite 900-D
New York City 10017
Tel: 212-687-9554 / 800-927-9554
Fax: 212-573-9731

South African Tourism Board
500 Fifth Avenue, 20th floor
New York City 10110
212-730-2929 phone
212-764-1980 fax
e-mail: Satourny@aol.com

Moroccan National Tourist Office
20 East 46th Street
New York City 10017
212-557-2520
Fax 212-949-8148

Jamaica Tourist Board
801 Second Avenue
New York, NY 10017
Tel: 212-856-9727 or 1-800-233-4582
Fax 212-856-9730

Puerto Rico Tourism Company
PO Box 902-3960
San Juan, Puerto Rico 00902-3960
Tel: 787-721-2400
Fax: 787-725-4417

Appendix C
Airlines & Cruise Lines

Airlines

American Airlines
150 East 42nd St., 4th floor
New York City 10017
Phone 212-476-9521
Fax 212-476-9557
e-mail: lance_magee@amrcorp.com

Air Jamaica Limited
95-25 Queens Blvd.
Rego Park, NY 11374
Reservations 800-523-5585

Royal Air Moroccan
Moroccan International Airlines
55 East 59th Street, Suite 178
New York City 10022-1112
212-750-5115
1-800-292-0081
Fax 212-754-4215
Reservations: 212-750-6071
1-800-344-6726

Air Afrique
1350 Avenue of the Americas
New York City 10019
212-586-5908
1-800-456-9192

Varig Brazilian Airlines
71 South Central Avenue
Valley Stream, NY 11580
Tel: 516-612-0366
Fax: 516-612-0235
Reservations: 800-468-2744
e-mail: nycvrg8@aol.com

Ghana Airways
Reservations: 1-800-404-4262

Cruise Lines

Sonesta Nile Cruises
4, El Tayaran St.
Nasr City, Cairo, Egypt
Tel: 202-2628111
Fax 202-264-1201

Appendix D
Hotels and Resorts

Catassaba Hotel
Alamedas da Praia, 101
Itapua - CEP- 41600-270
Salvador, Bahia, Brazil
Tel: 071-374-0555
Fax: 071-374-4849

Le Meridien Copacabana Hotel Rio
Av. Atlantica, 1.020 - CEP 22010-000
Rio de Janeiro, Brazil
Tel: 021-275-9922
Fax: 21-542-6739
e-mail: sales@meridien-br.com

Oberoi Hotel Egypt
Hotel Mena House Oberoi
Pyramids Road
Giza, Cairo, Egypt
Tel: 3833222
Fax: 3837777
e-mai: obmhosm@oberoi.com.eg

San Juan Grand Beach Resort & Casino
PO Box 6676
San Juan, Puerto Rico 00914-6676
800-544-3008
www.sjgrand.com

The Buccaneer Hotel
Box 25200Gallows Bay
St. Croix, U.S.V.I. 00824
Tel: 340-773-2100
Fax: 340-773-0010
www.thebuccaneer.com

The Grace Hotel in Rosebank
54 Bath Avenue, 2196 Rosebank
PO Box 2536, Parklands, South Africa
Tel: 011-280-7300
Fax: 011-280-7333
e-mail: graceres@grace.co.za

Appendix E
Convention Centers

Bahiatursa
Jardim Armacao
Centro de Convencoes da Bahia
CEP (Zip Code) 41750-270
Tel: 55(71) 370-8593
Fax: 55 (71) 370-8697
Salvador Bahia Brasil

Rio convention & Visitors Bureau
Rua Visconde de Piraja, 547 - 6th floor
22415-900
Ipanema - Rio de Janeiro - Brazil
Tel: 5521-259-6165
Fax: 5521-511-2592
e-mail:rcvb@embratel.net.br
www.rioconventionbureau.com.br

Haggins International Tours Puts A Little Show-Bizzz In Travel

Haggins International Tours opens your eyes to the world and allows you to dream and travel to many exotic destinations around the world. Haggins International Tours is a customized group tour company that specializes in affordable and personalized tours to Africa and Brazil. H.I.T. was established in 1991 and is owned and operated by Jon Haggins.

The minimum group size is thirty participants. Collectively, the group is an ideal situation for single persons to venture out. This opportunity allows them to meet others with similar interests. Sometimes they bond for life.

H.I.T. loves a challenging task, such as a Church or Convention group traveling with children. Special educational and cultural programs can be arranged for children.

Haggins International Tours offers affordable packages, based on double occupancy, include roundtrip air, transfers, baggage handling, deluxe hotels, some meals, some tours and an English-speaking guide.

Haggins personalizes tours and allows that allow you to understand other cultures. He also sets a little time aside so that you can smell the roses.

Haggins International Tours specializes in personalized group tours to exotic destinations around the world.

Expand your horizons by participating in H.I.T.'s Black Heritage Tours to Africa & Brazil, Benin, Burkina Faso, Egypt, Gambia, Ghana, Ivory Coast, Kenya, Mali, Morocco, South Africa and more.

For more information, contact: Jon Haggins, Haggins International Tours, P.O. Box 20902, New York, NY 10023, email: or call: 212-319-2894

About the Author

Jon Haggins is the executive producer and host of Travel & Dining Tips with Jon Haggins, a half-hour weekly television show. He has contributed several short inspirational stories to Eric Copage's *Soul Food* book. And is presently the food and travel editor for the Amsterdam News and travel editor for *Luxe Magazine,* a new upscale lifestyle publication. Jon has been a fashion designer, fashion show producer, cabaret singer, product spokesperson and tour operator.

Jon started his first career as a fashion designer in the mid 1960's, shortly after graduating from the Fashion Institute of Technology in New York City. Every national fashion magazine and newspaper featured his designs. *Women's Wear Daily, New York Times,* and *Vogue* were the first to feature his designs. Bill Cunningham, then a reporter for the Chicago Tribune, in the early 70's, wrote about one of Jon's designs. He referred to it as "The Dress of the Year." The dress sold 1,000 units per week in every department and specialty store across the country.

Jon's fashions have been worn by many celebrities such as: Diana Ross, Helen Gurley Brown, Sheryl Lee Ralph, Debbie Allen, Felicia Rashad, Racquel Welch, Diahann Carroll, Lynn Redgrave, etc. Moreover, he has lectured to more than 15,000 fashion students from around the country. Cornell University, in Itacha New York, honored him with a month long exhibition of his designs. Jon has also designed costumes for several Off-Broadway shows and several Soap Operas.

Then Jon became a cabaret singer followed by corporate spokesperson for a fortune 500 company. He was an invited guest speaker at the Smithsonian Museum in Washington D.C. and Master of Ceremony for the Culture-Fest fashion show in Abidjan, Ivory Coast. Jon produced a fashion show in Ghana for ATA/Revlon and Ghana's president, Jerry Rawlings. He is also the president of Haggins International Tours, which was formed in 1991.

Jon has appeared on many TV and Radio talk shows such as: "Regis & Kathie Lee", "The McCleary Hour", "Daybreak—CNN", "Geraldo", "Saturday Tribune-Phil", "Evening Magazine", "Midday-Live", "Sunday Classics with Hal Jackson", "Breakfast Cort with Sean Cort, etc.

Haggins International Tours, editorials have appeared in *The New York Times, NY Newsday, Amsterdam News, The Daily News, The Chicago Tribune, Florida Today, The Washington Post, Boston Globe, The Bergen Record, The Dallas News, The Tennessean, Los Angeles Times, Los Angeles Daily News, San Francisco Examiner, Houston Chronicle, Charlotte Post, Essence, Heart & Soul, Black Enterprise* and *Black Elegance Magazines* etc.

ORDER FORM
WWW.AMBERBOOKS.COM
African-American Self Help and Career Books

Fax Orders:	480-283-0991	Postal Orders: Send Checks & Money Orders to:
Telephone Orders:	480-460-1660	Amber Books Publishing
Online Orders: E-mail:	Amberbks@aol.com	1334 E. Chandler Blvd., Suite 5-D67
		Phoenix, AZ 85048

_____ *The African-American Travel Guide*

_____ *Beautiful Black Hair: A Step-by-Step Instructional Guide*

_____ *How to Get Rich When You Ain't Got Nothing*

_____ *Suge Knight: The Rise, Fall, and Rise of Death Row Records*

_____ *The African-American Teenagers Guide to Personal Growth, Health, Safety, Sex and Survival*

_____ *Get That Cutie in Commercials, Televisions, Films & Videos*

_____ *Wake Up and Smell the Dollars! Whose Inner City is This Anyway?*

_____ *How to Own and Operate Your Home Day Care Business Successfully Without Going Nuts!*

_____ *The African-American Woman's Guide to Successful Make-up and Skin Care*

_____ *How to Play the Sports Recruiting Game and Get an Athletic Scholarship:*
The Handbook and Guide to Success for the African-American High School Student-Athlete

_____ *Is Modeling for You? The Handbook and Guide for the Young Aspiring Black Model*

Name:_____

Company Name:_____

Address:_____

City:_____State:_____ Zip:_____

Telephone: (_____) _____E-mail:_____

For Bulk Rates Call: **480-460-1660**   ## ORDER NOW

Beautiful Black Hair	$16.95	❏ Check ❏ Money Order ❏ Cashiers Check
How to Get Rich	$14.95	❏ Credit Card: ❏ MC ❏ Visa ❏ Amex ❏ Discover
Travel Guide	$14.95	
Suge Knight	$21.95	CC#_____
Teenagers Guide	$19.95	
Cutie in Commercials	$16.95	Expiration Date:_____
Wake Up & Smell the Dollars	$18.95	**Payable to:**
Home Day Care	$12.95	Amber Books
Successful Make-up	$14.95	1334 E. Chandler Blvd., Suite 5-D67
Sports Recruiting:	$12.95	Phoenix, AZ 85048
Modeling:	$14.95	**Shipping:** $5.00 per book. Allow 7 days for delivery.
		Sales Tax: Add 7.05% to books shipped to Arizona addresses.
		Total enclosed: $_____